MOCKT[illegible]S

& CANAPÉS

MOCKTAILS

STEP BY STEP
AN
EASY
GUIDE

& CANAPÉS

GELDING STREET PRESS

CONTENTS

50 **ORIGINAL FRESH**
redcurrant and soda

51 **LUSCIOUS LEMON**
rockmelon and coriander

52 **TART AND TANGY**
mustard, grapefruit and apple

53 **THREE LITTLE BIRDS**
pineapple, fig and coconut

54 **NICE AND PEACHY**
with cherries and apricots

55 **REFRESH**
cucumber, apple and chilli

56 **VIRGIN LIGHT COLADA**
coconut and pineapple

57 **FLORENTINE**
apple, cucumber and tarragon

58 **BETTY BOOP**
strawberry, cucumber and pear

59 **GREEN SMOOTHIE**
avocado, apple and kiwifruit

60 **WELCOME TO PARADISE**
beetroot, passionfruit and raspberry

61 **DO BRAZIL**
pineapple, passionfruit and orange

62 **INFERNO KISS**
capsicum, strawberry and spices

63 **CINNAMON SERENITY**
clementine, pear and cinnamon

64 **FABULOUS RIO**
passionfruit and caramelised pineapple

65 **PEACH SUNSET**
apricot, peach and orange

66 **KIWI CUCUMBER**
cooler

67 **MAJORELLE'S GARDEN**
green tea and floral water

68 **ACAI DELIGHT**
strawberry and basil

69 **DAISY DELIGHT**
cucumber and lychee

70 **SAN ITALIA**
orange and grapefruit

71 **FRESH GREEN TEA**
grapes, lime and birch

72 **MOCKTAIL RIO**
fruit and spices

73 **PUSSYFOOT JOHNSON**
citrus and grenadine

74 **BILLABONG**
strawberry, lychee and melon

75 **SPICED**
Milky Way

FINGER FOOD

INTRODUCTION

WE BELIEVE MAKING MOCKTAILS SHOULD BE HASSLE FREE, SO WE'VE PREPARED 80 CLASSIC AND CREATIVE RECIPES TO MAKE IN A FLASH.

Are you keen to make alcohol-free cocktails to enjoy with friends but don't have the time to get your head around long-winded instructions? Feel like testing the cocktail shaker you were gifted but don't have any recipe ideas? Hosting friends who don't drink and want to impress them with something beyond soda and juice? This mocktail cookbook is your go-to guide for crafting delicious, alcohol-free drinks that are anything but boring.

With easy-to-follow recipes and a few clever tricks, you'll be whipping up vibrant, refreshing, and gourmet mocktails in no time. Whether you're after something fruity, exotic, spicy, sparkling, or still, there's a perfect pour for every occasion: by the glass or the jug. Get ready to shake, stir, and sip your way through the night!

What's a pre-dinner drink without something to nibble on? So we've also included 21 savoury finger food recipes to delight your tastebuds and pair perfectly with your mocktails.

THE FORMULA IS SIMPLE: there are no long instructions in this book, just the essentials. Add the +, follow the → and, as surely as 1 + 1 = 2, you will work wonders with these 101 recipes. Follow the images and you'll make the recipe. Welcome to cooking step by step without the hassle!

01 BUNNY RABBIT

carrot, pear and passionfruit

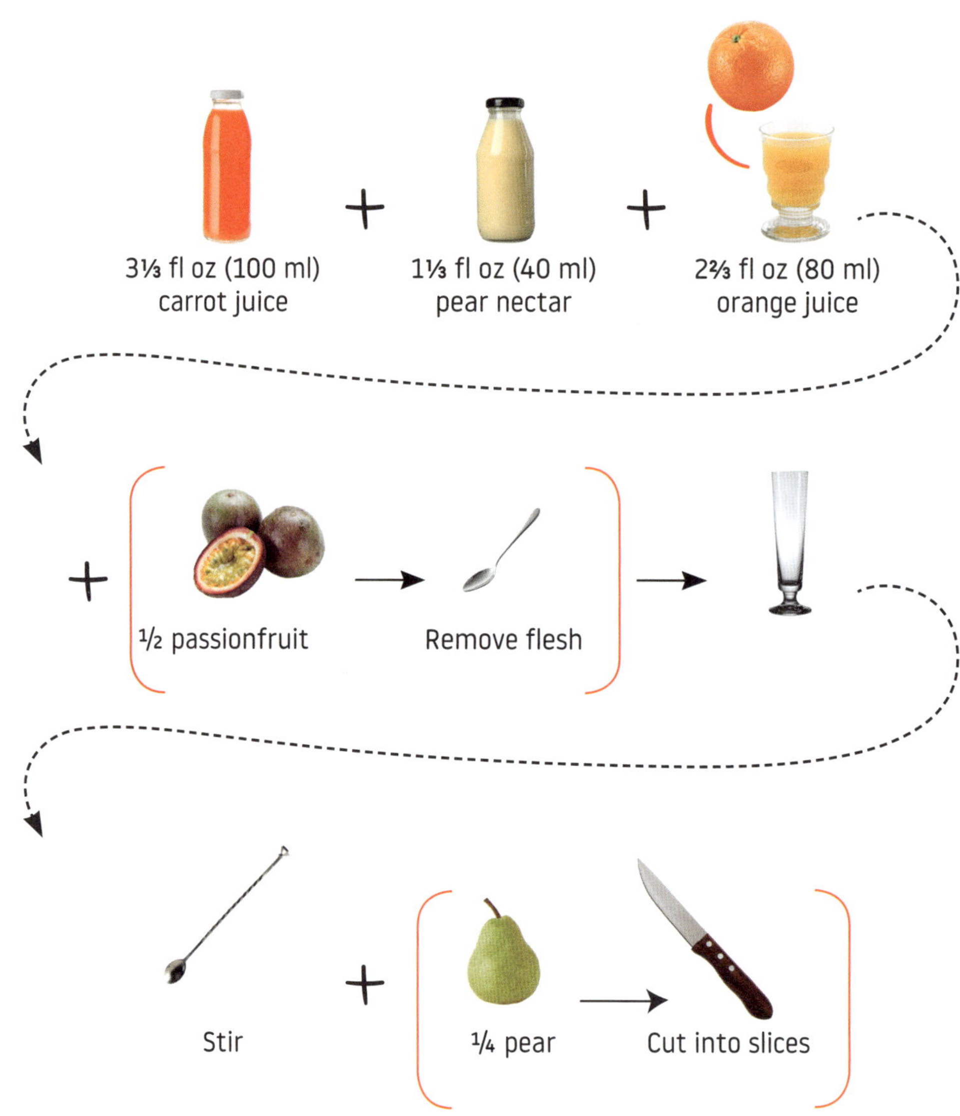

3⅓ fl oz (100 ml) carrot juice
1⅓ fl oz (40 ml) pear nectar
2⅔ fl oz (80 ml) orange juice
½ passionfruit
Remove flesh
Stir
¼ pear
Cut into slices

MAKES 1 GLASS
PREPARATION: 5 MINUTES

- 3⅓ fl oz (100 ml) carrot juice
- 1⅓ fl oz (40 ml) pear nectar
- 2⅔ fl oz (80 ml) orange juice
- ½ passionfruit, flesh removed
- ¼ pear, sliced

02 CITRUS REFRESHER

citrus and cranberry

1 scoop lemon sorbet
⅔ fl oz (20 ml) cane sugar syrup
½ pink grapefruit
1 clementine or mandarin, juiced
3⅓ fl oz (100 ml) cranberry juice
Crushed ice
20 SECONDS
Blend 20 seconds

MAKES 1 GLASS
PREPARATION: 5 MINUTES

- 1 scoop lemon sorbet
- ⅔ fl oz (20 ml) cane sugar syrup
- ½ pink grapefruit, juiced
- 1 clementine or mandarin, juiced
- 3⅓ fl oz (100 ml) cranberry juice
- crushed ice

03 CHARLIE BABY

white grapes and strawberries

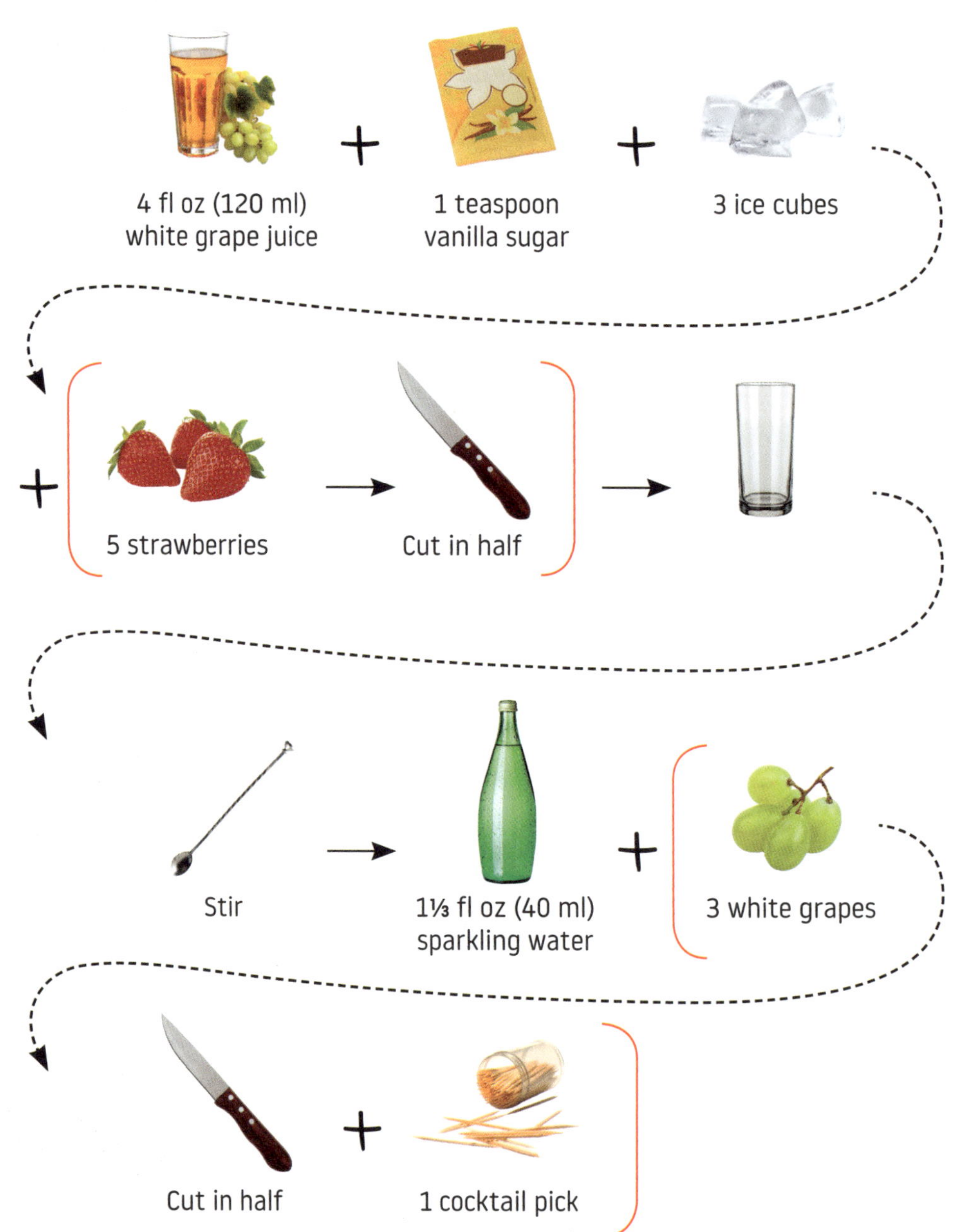

4 fl oz (120 ml)
white grape juice
1 teaspoon
vanilla sugar
3 ice cubes
5 strawberries
Cut in half
Stir
1⅓ fl oz (40 ml)
sparkling water
3 white grapes
Cut in half
1 cocktail pick

MAKES 1 GLASS
PREPARATION: 5 MINUTES

- 4 fl oz (120 ml) white grape juice
- 1 teaspoon vanilla sugar
- 3 ice cubes
- 5 strawberries, halved
- 1⅓ fl oz (40 ml) sparkling water
- 3 white grapes, halved

04 MEXICAN STYLE

citrus, bergamot and avocado

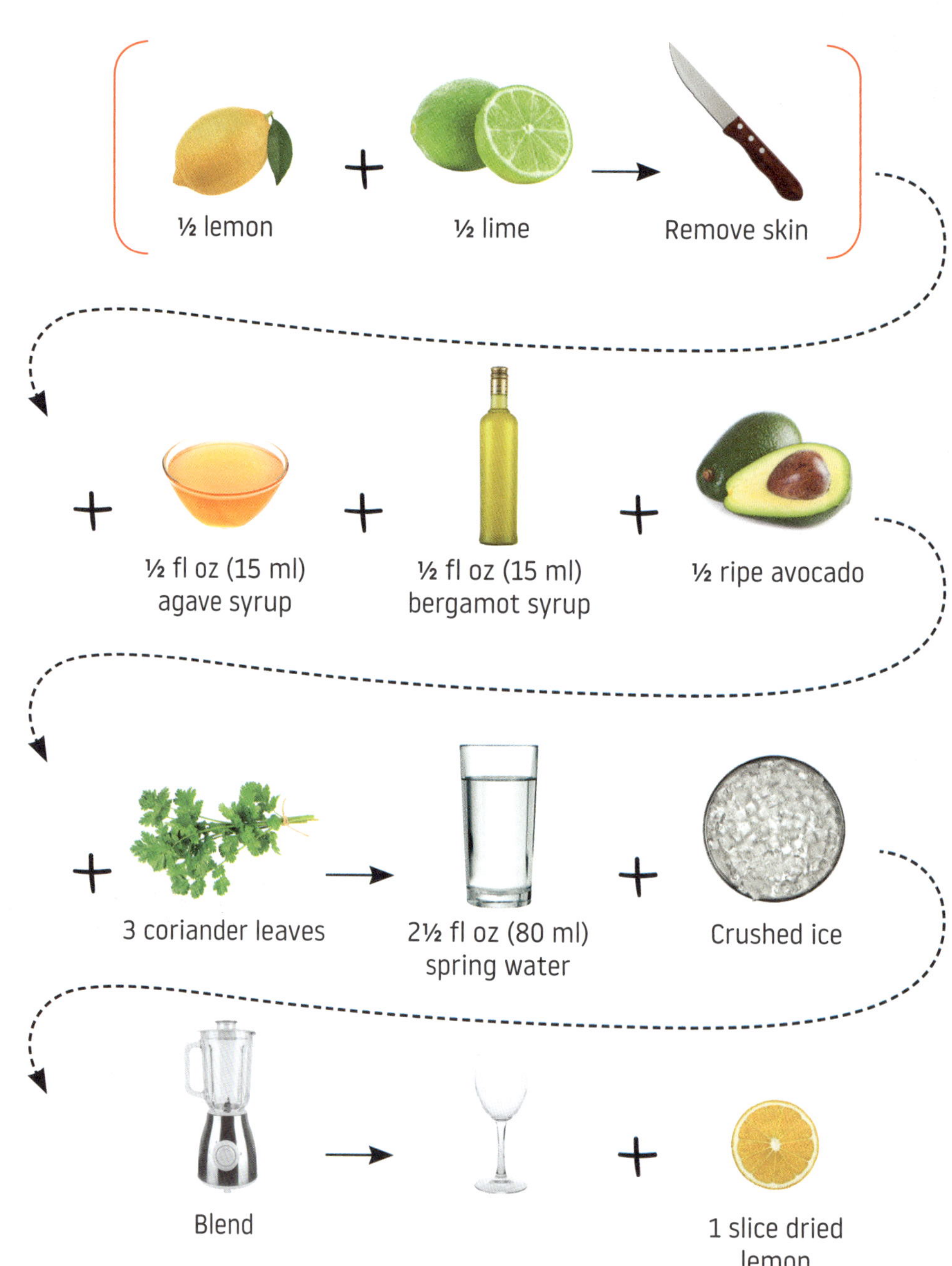

½ lemon
½ lime
Remove skin
½ fl oz (15 ml) agave syrup
½ fl oz (15 ml) bergamot syrup
½ ripe avocado
3 coriander leaves
2½ fl oz (80 ml) spring water
Crushed ice
Blend
1 slice dried lemon

MAKES 1 GLASS
PREPARATION: 5 MINUTES

- ½ lemon
- ½ lime
- ½ fl oz (15 ml) agave syrup
- ½ fl oz (15 ml) bergamot syrup
- ½ ripe avocado
- 3 coriander leaves
- 2½ fl oz (80 ml) spring water
- crushed ice
- 1 slice dried lemon (optional)

05 LIKE A VIRGIN

orange, cranberry and lemonade

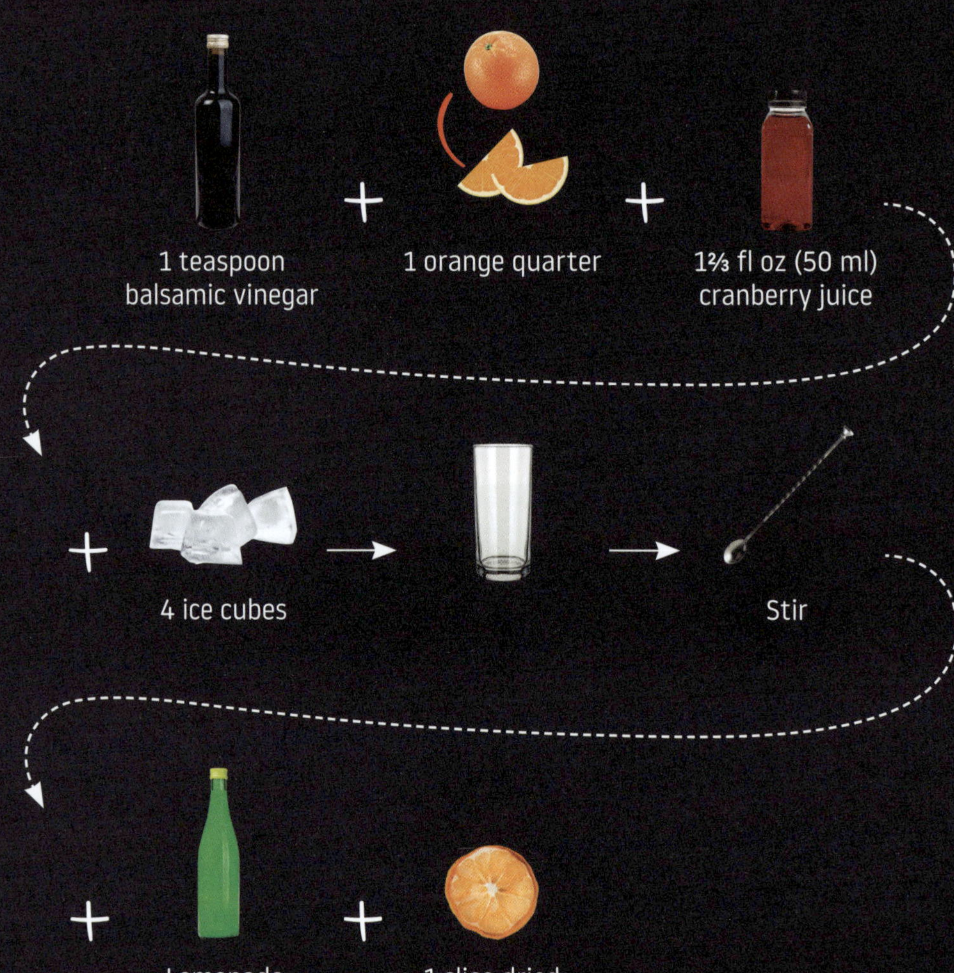
1 teaspoon balsamic vinegar
1 orange quarter
1⅔ fl oz (50 ml) cranberry juice
4 ice cubes
Stir
Lemonade
1 slice dried orange

MAKES 1 GLASS
PREPARATION: 5 MINUTES

- 1 teaspoon balsamic vinegar
- 1 orange quarter
- 1⅔ fl oz (50 ml) cranberry juice
- 4 ice cubes
- lemonade
- 1 slice dried orange

06 PANAME

mango, pineapple and passionfruit

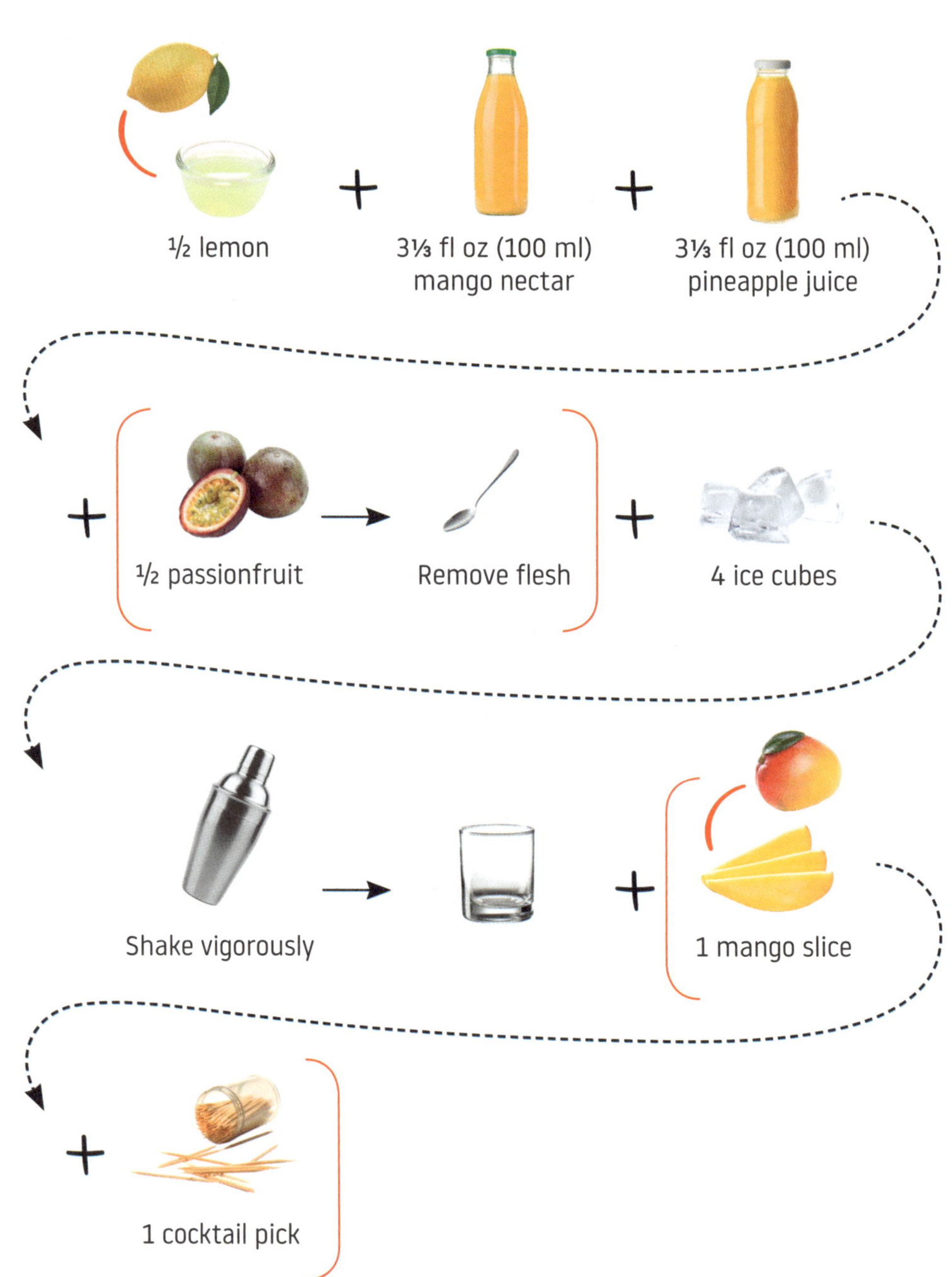

½ lemon
3⅓ fl oz (100 ml) mango nectar
3⅓ fl oz (100 ml) pineapple juice
½ passionfruit
Remove flesh
4 ice cubes
Shake vigorously
1 mango slice
1 cocktail pick

MAKES 1 GLASS
PREPARATION: 5 MINUTES

- ½ lemon, juiced
- 3⅓ fl oz (100 ml) mango nectar
- 3⅓ fl oz (100 ml) pineapple juice
- ½ passionfruit, flesh removed
- 4 ice cubes
- 1 mango slice

07 VIRGIN BLOODY MARY

tomato and rocket

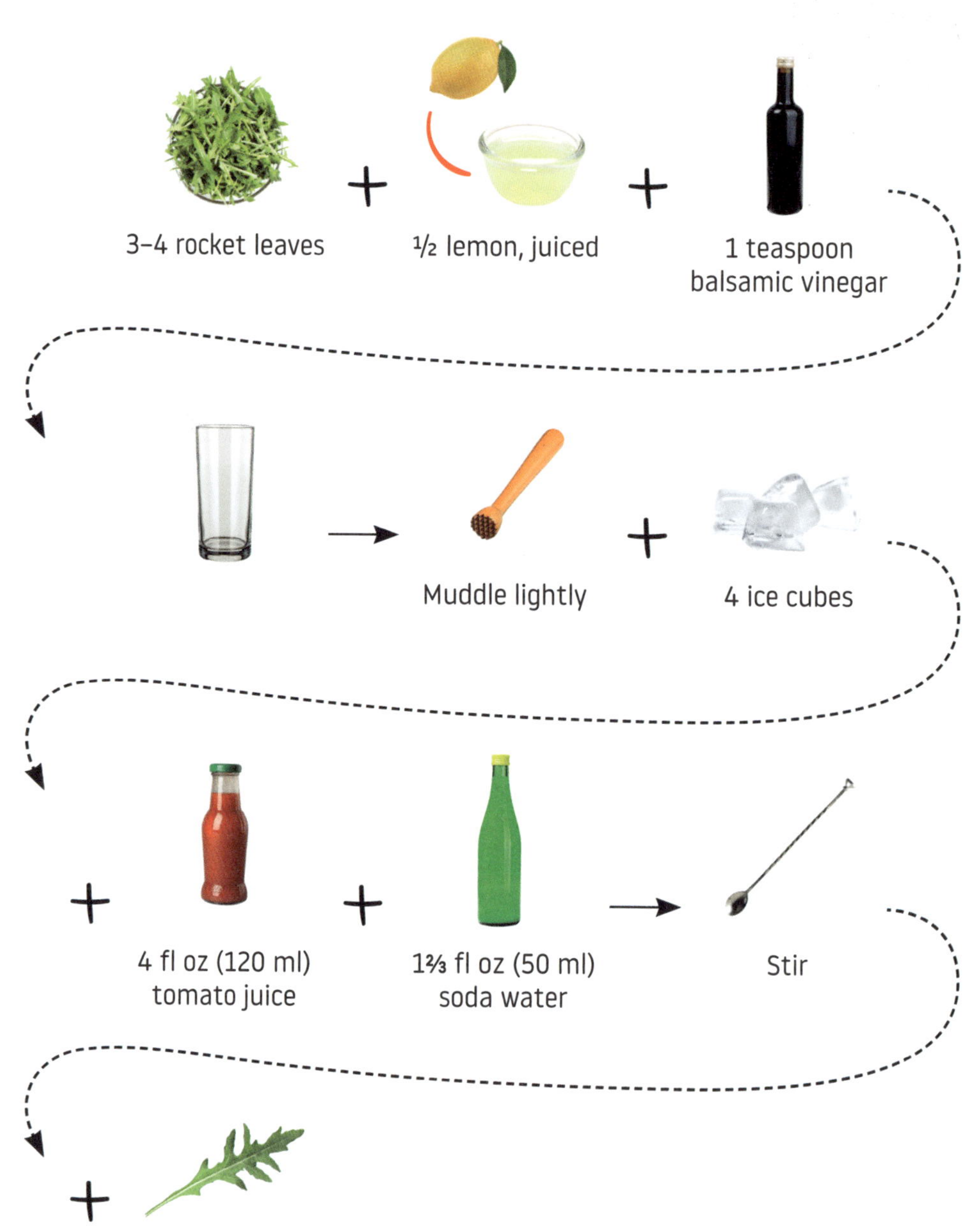
3–4 rocket leaves
½ lemon, juiced
1 teaspoon balsamic vinegar
Muddle lightly
4 ice cubes
4 fl oz (120 ml) tomato juice
1⅔ fl oz (50 ml) soda water
Stir

MAKES 1 GLASS
PREPARATION: 5 MINUTES

- 4 or 5 rocket leaves
- ½ lemon, juiced
- 1 teaspoon balsamic vinegar
- 4 ice cubes
- 4 fl oz (120 ml) tomato juice
- 1⅔ fl oz (50 ml) soda water

08 GINGER
lemonade

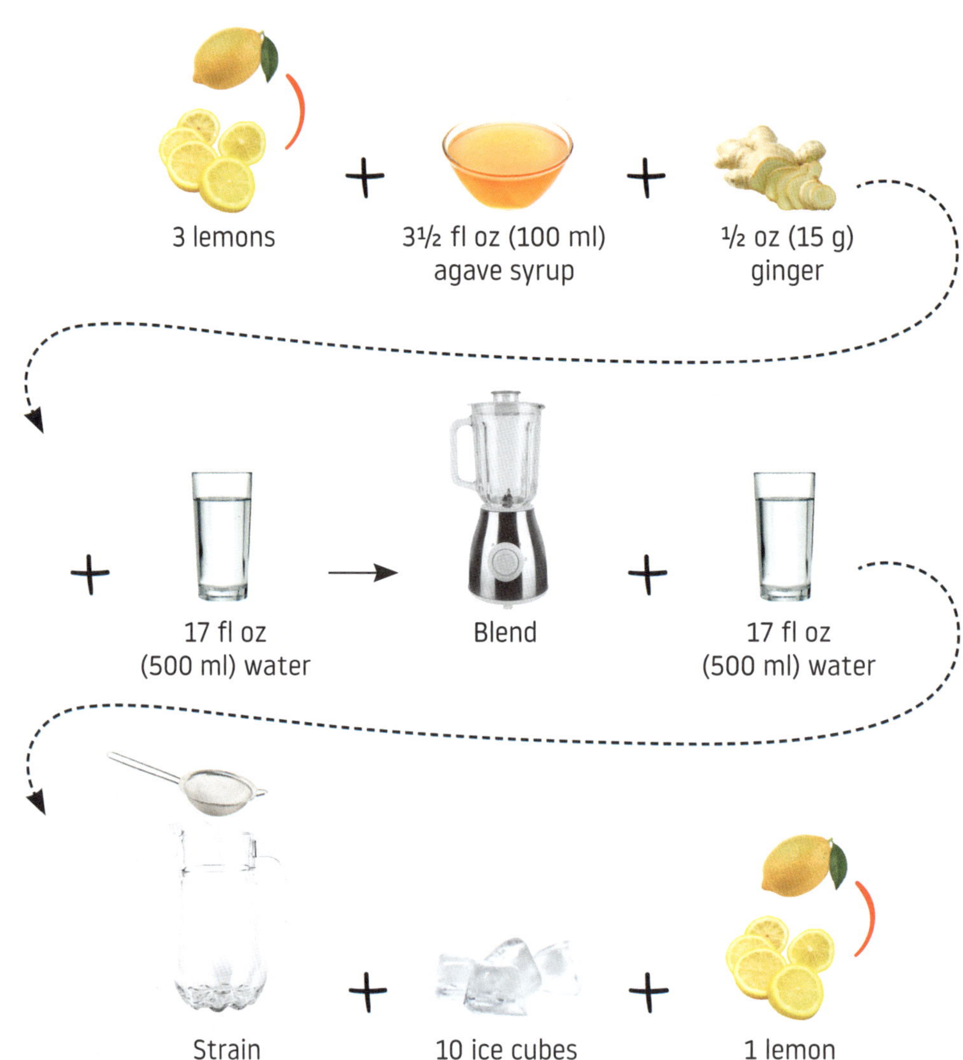
3 lemons
3½ fl oz (100 ml) agave syrup
½ oz (15 g) ginger
17 fl oz (500 ml) water
Blend
17 fl oz (500 ml) water
Strain
10 ice cubes
1 lemon

MAKES 37 FL OZ (1.1 LITRES)
PREPARATION: 10 MINUTES

- 4 lemons, sliced
- 3⅓ fl oz (100 ml) agave syrup
- ½ oz (15 g) ginger
- 34 fl oz (1 l) water
- 10 ice cubes

09 PRETTY GOOD THING

fruit and ginger

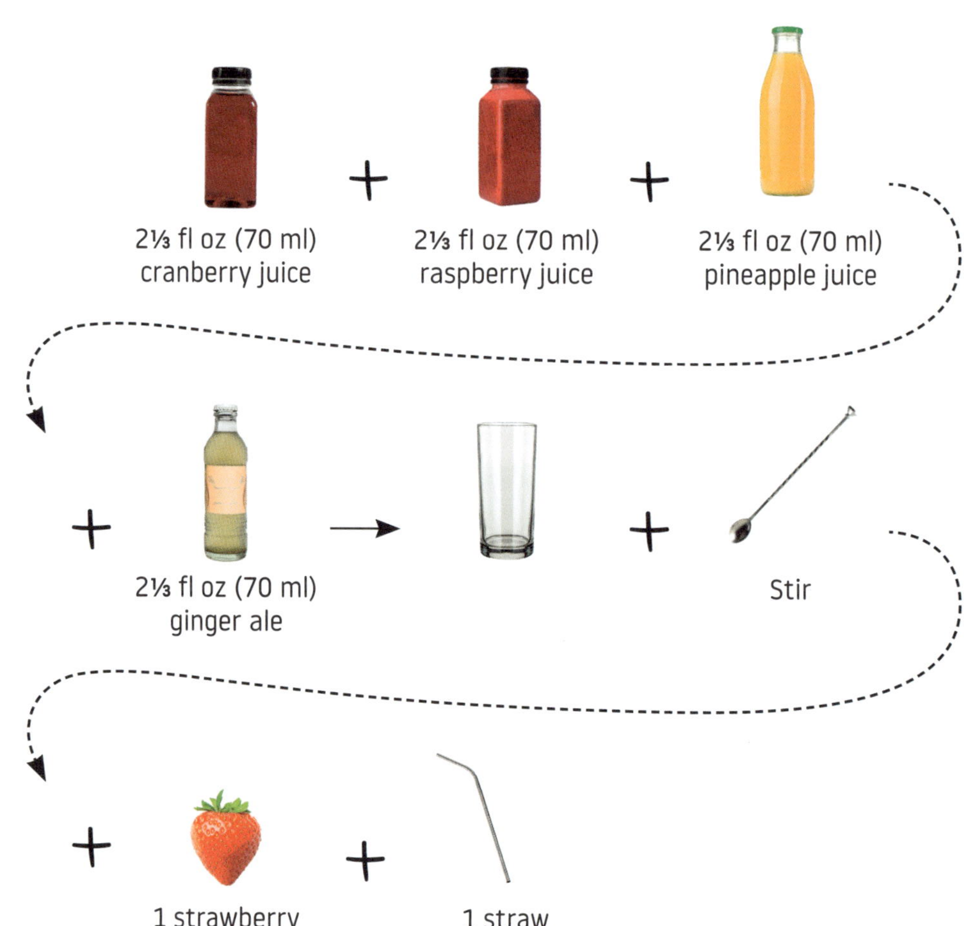

2⅓ fl oz (70 ml)
cranberry juice
2⅓ fl oz (70 ml)
raspberry juice
2⅓ fl oz (70 ml)
pineapple juice
2⅓ fl oz (70 ml)
ginger ale
Stir
1 strawberry
1 straw

MAKES 1 GLASS
PREPARATION: 5 MINUTES

- 2⅓ fl oz (70 ml) cranberry juice
- 2⅓ fl oz (70 ml) raspberry juice
- 2⅓ fl oz (70 ml) pineapple juice
- 2⅓ fl oz (70 ml) ginger ale
- 1 strawberry

10 KAWAII

lychee and hibiscus

10 MINUTES
3 dried hibiscus flowers
17 fl oz (500 ml) boiling water
Leave to infuse 10 minutes
Strain
20 MINUTES
Leave to cool 20 minutes
Remove 3⅓ fl oz (100 ml)
4 ice cubes
3 tinned lychees
⅔ fl oz (20 ml) syrup from tin
Stir

MAKES 1 GLASS
PREPARATION: 5 MINUTES
COOKING: 2 MINUTES
RESTING: 30 MINUTES

- 3 dried hibiscus flowers
- 17 fl oz (500 ml) boiling water
- 4 ice cubes
- 3 tinned lychees + ⅔ fl oz (20 ml) syrup from tin

11 DAIRY-FREE MILKSHAKE

peach, banana and cinnamon

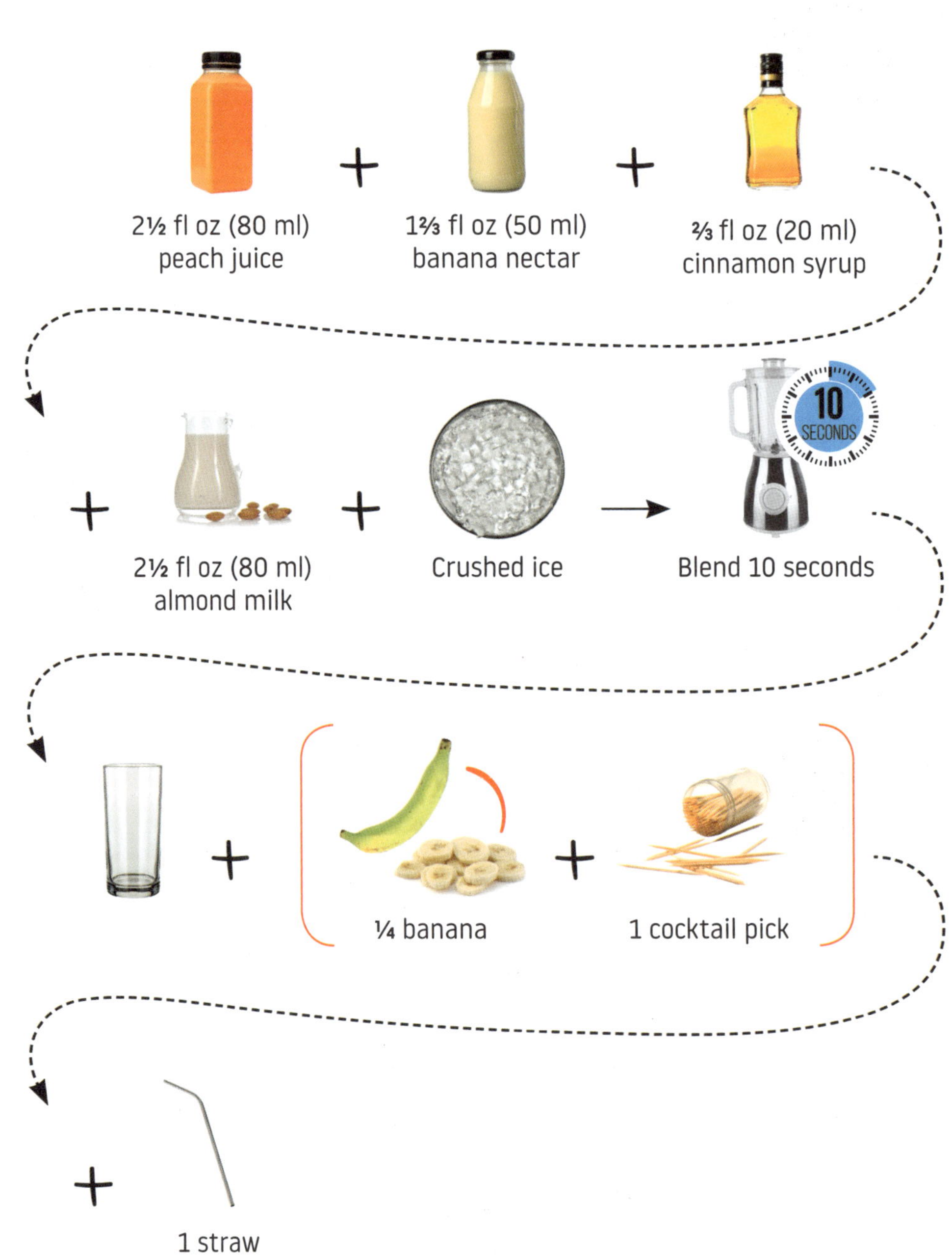
2½ fl oz (80 ml)
peach juice
1⅔ fl oz (50 ml)
banana nectar
⅔ fl oz (20 ml)
cinnamon syrup
2½ fl oz (80 ml)
almond milk
Crushed ice
10
SECONDS
Blend 10 seconds
¼ banana
1 cocktail pick
1 straw

MAKES 1 GLASS
PREPARATION: 5 MINUTES

- 2½ fl oz (80 ml) peach juice
- 1⅔ fl oz (50 ml) banana nectar
- ⅔ fl oz (20 ml) cinnamon syrup
- 2½ fl oz (80 ml) almond milk
- crushed ice
- ¼ banana, sliced

12 HEAVY DUTY

cranberry, hibiscus and capsicum

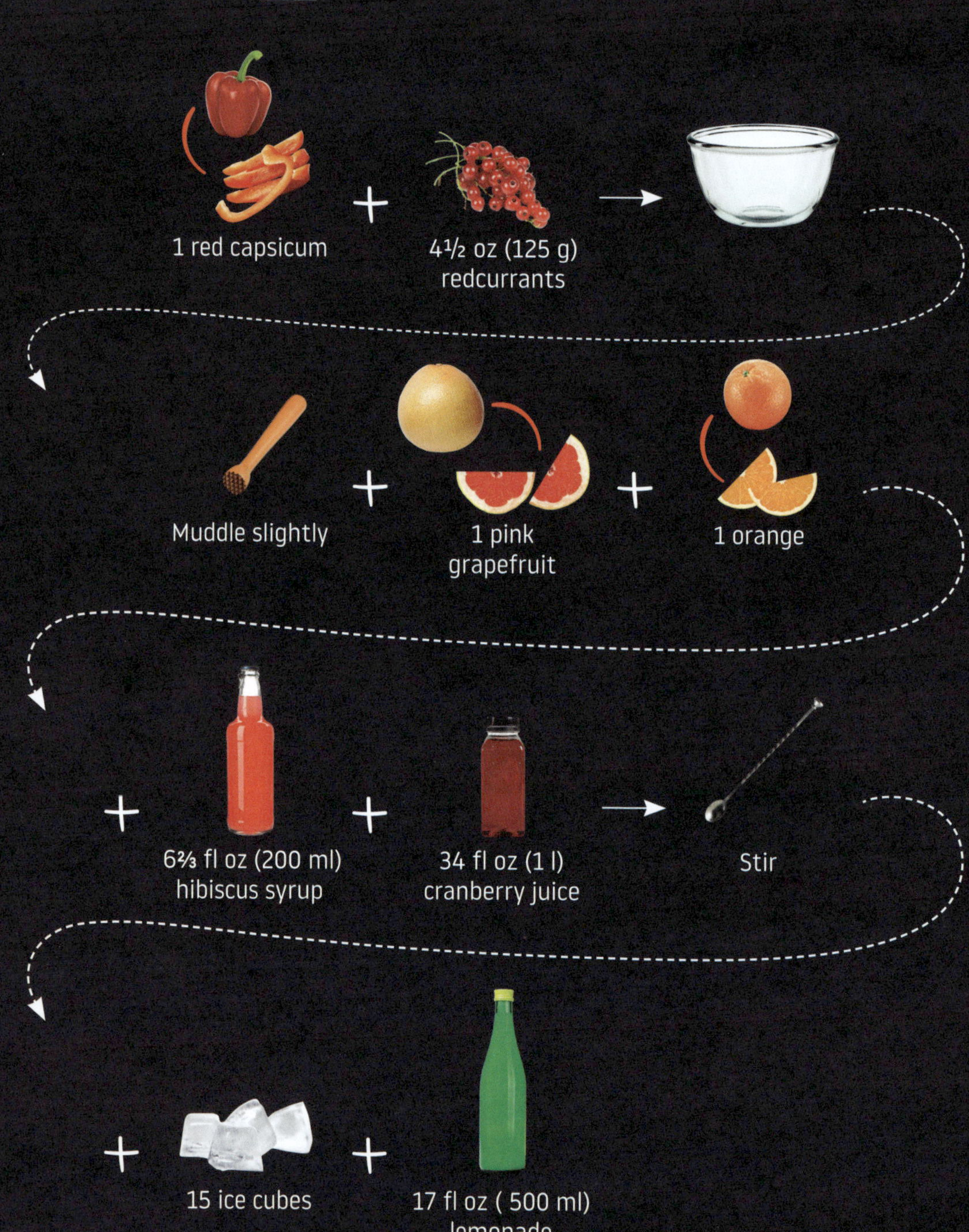

1 red capsicum
+
4½ oz (125 g)
redcurrants
Muddle slightly
+
1 pink
grapefruit
+
1 orange
+
6⅔ fl oz (200 ml)
hibiscus syrup
+
34 fl oz (1 l)
cranberry juice
Stir
+
15 ice cubes
+
17 fl oz (500 ml)
lemonade

MAKES 60 FL OZ (1.7 LITRES)
PREPARATION: 10 MINUTES

- 1 red capsicum, cut into strips
- 4½ oz (125 g) redcurrants
- 1 pink grapefruit, cut into half slices
- 1 orange, cut into half slices
- 6⅔ fl oz (200 ml) hibiscus syrup
- 34 fl oz (1 l) cranberry juice
- 15 ice cubes
- 17 fl oz (500 ml) lemonade

13 SUMMER REFRESH

watermelon, strawberries and mint

2¾ oz (80 g) watermelon
Blend
Strain
6 strawberries
1 sprig mint
Blend
2–3 mint leaves
1 straw

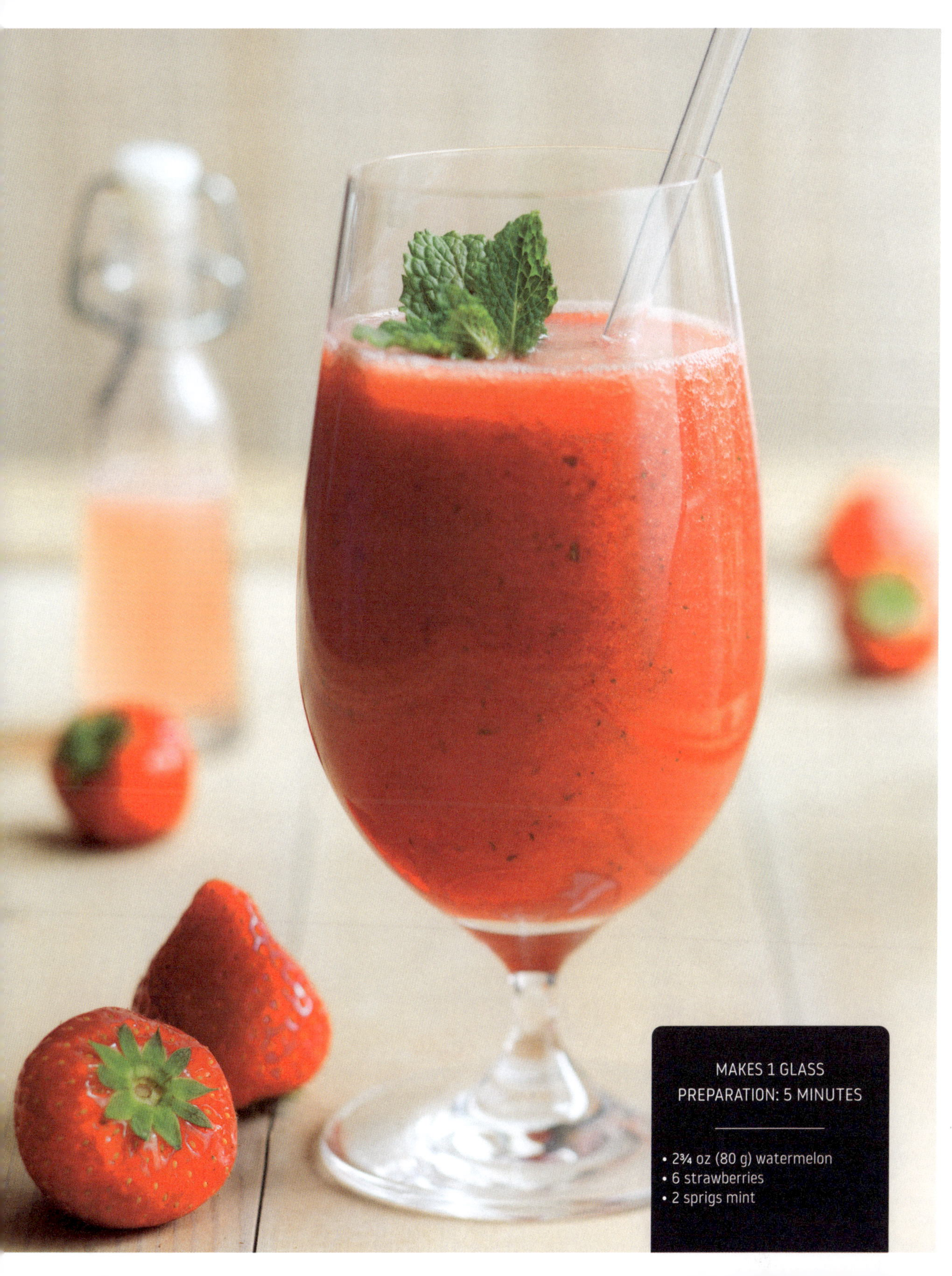

MAKES 1 GLASS
PREPARATION: 5 MINUTES

- 2¾ oz (80 g) watermelon
- 6 strawberries
- 2 sprigs mint

14 VIRGIN *mojito*

½ cucumber
Blitz
Juice of ½ lime
Strain
1 sprig mint
3 cucumber sticks
1 dash
mint syrup
Crushed ice
Sparkling water

MAKES 1 GLASS
PREPARATION: 5 MINUTES

- ½ cucumber, chopped + 3 sticks
- ½ lime, juiced
- 1 sprig mint
- 1 dash mint syrup
- crushed ice
- sparkling water

15 POMELO *mojito*

½ pink pomelo
7 mint leaves
1 tablespoon honey
Muddle
3 ice cubes
3⅓ fl oz (100 ml) Schweppes® Agrum Citrus Blend (or orange soda)
1 sprig mint

MAKES 1 GLASS
PREPARATION: 5 MINUTES

- ½ pink pomelo, sliced
- 7 mint leaves + 1 sprig
- 1 tablespoon honey
- 3 ice cubes
- 3⅓ fl oz (100 ml) Schweppes® Agrum Citrus Blend (or orange soda)

16 VIRGIN CUCUMBER

mojito

10 mint leaves
½ lime
4 small pieces cucumber
SUCRE DE CANNE
2⅓ fl oz (20 ml) cane sugar syrup
Muddle
Crushed ice
2½ fl oz (80 ml) sparkling water
1 cucumber slice
3 mint leaves

MAKES 1 GLASS
PREPARATION: 5 MINUTES

- 13 mint leaves
- ½ lime
- 4 small pieces cucumber + 1 slice
- 2⅓ fl oz (20 ml) cane sugar syrup
- crushed ice
- 2½ fl oz (80 ml) sparkling water

17 BEACH BOOST

mango, coconut and pineapple

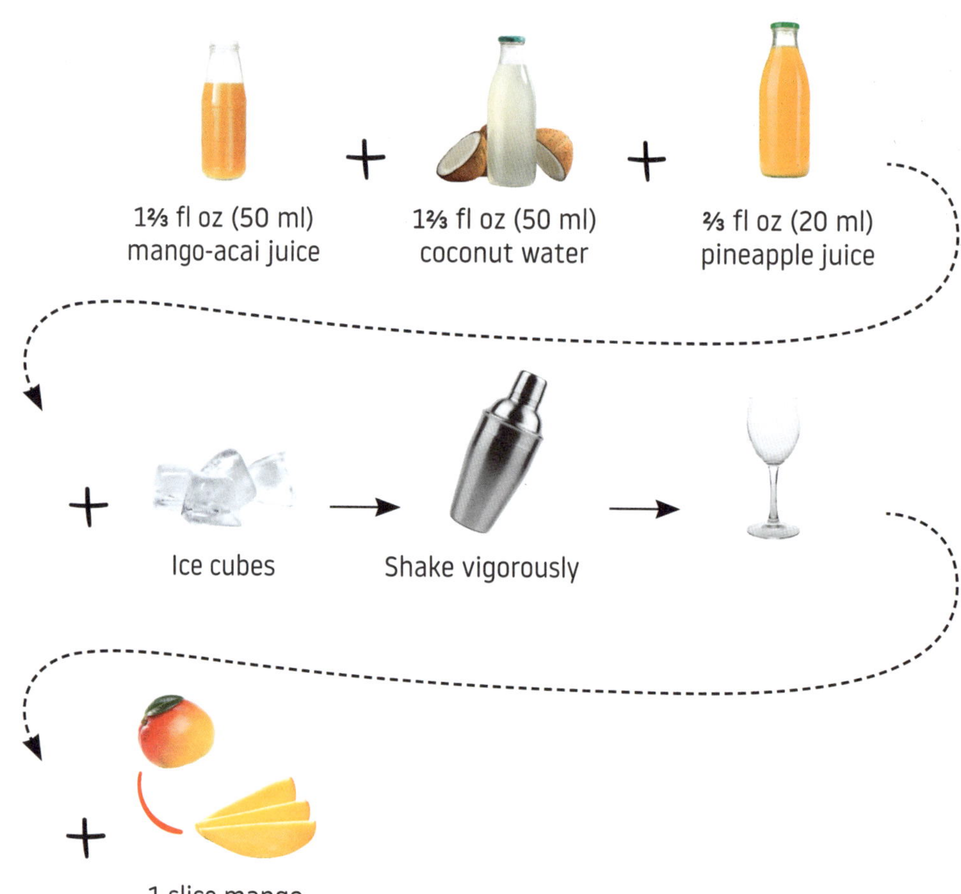

1⅔ fl oz (50 ml) mango-acai juice
1⅔ fl oz (50 ml) coconut water
⅔ fl oz (20 ml) pineapple juice
Ice cubes
Shake vigorously
1 slice mango

havaianas

MAKES 1 GLASS
PREPARATION: 5 MINUTES

- 1⅔ fl oz (50 ml) mango-acai juice
- 1⅔ fl oz (50 ml) coconut water
- ⅔ fl oz (20 ml) pineapple juice
- ice cubes
- 1 slice mango

18 ENERGISING

strawberry, banana and pear

A few almonds
½ banana
1⅓ fl oz (40 ml) strawberry juice
2 fl oz (60 ml) pear juice
Blend
3 ice cubes
1 tablespoon brewer's yeast

MAKES 1 GLASS
PREPARATION: 5 MINUTES

- a few almonds
- ½ banana, sliced
- 1⅓ fl oz (40 ml) strawberry juice
- 2 fl oz (60 ml) pear juice
- 3 ice cubes
- 1 tablespoon brewer's yeast

19 ORIENTAL CHIC

pomelo and capsicum

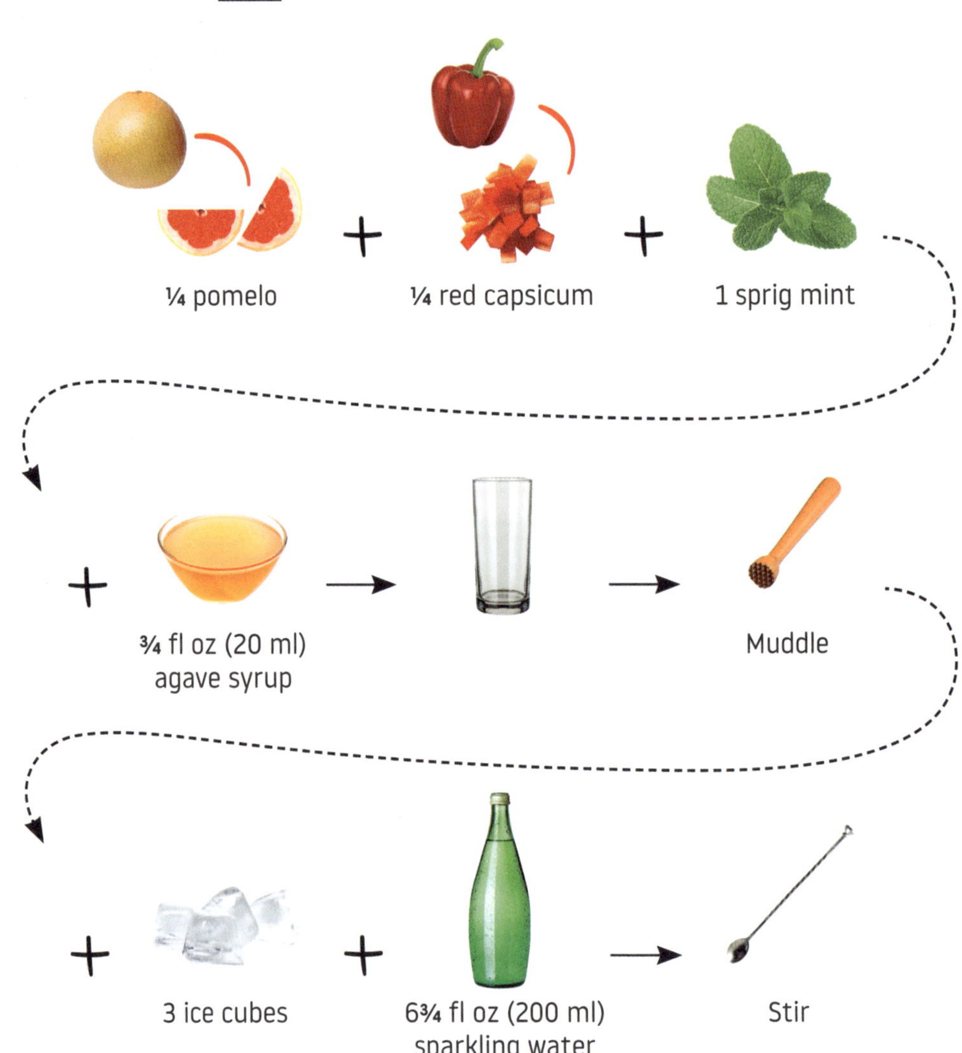
¼ pomelo
¼ red capsicum
1 sprig mint
¾ fl oz (20 ml)
agave syrup
Muddle
3 ice cubes
6¾ fl oz (200 ml)
sparkling water
Stir

MAKES 1 GLASS
PREPARATION: 5 MINUTES

- ¼ pomelo, skinned and diced
- ¼ red capsicum, diced
- 1 sprig mint
- ¾ fl oz (20 ml) agave syrup
- 3 ice cubes
- 6¾ fl oz (200 ml) sparkling water

20 FLORAL ORANGE

apricot, carrot and lavender

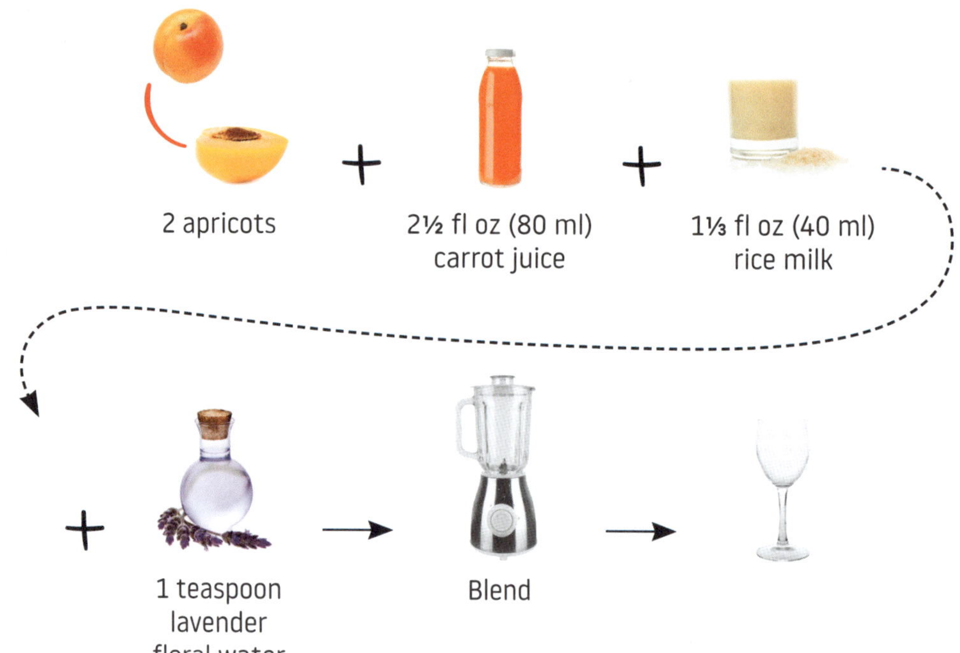
2 apricots
2½ fl oz (80 ml) carrot juice
1⅓ fl oz (40 ml) rice milk
1 teaspoon lavender floral water
Blend

MAKES 1 GLASS
PREPARATION: 5 MINUTES

- 2 apricots, seeded
- 2½ fl oz (80 ml) carrot juice
- 1⅓ fl oz (40 ml) rice milk
- 1 teaspoon lavender floral water

21 CRAZY *cucumber*

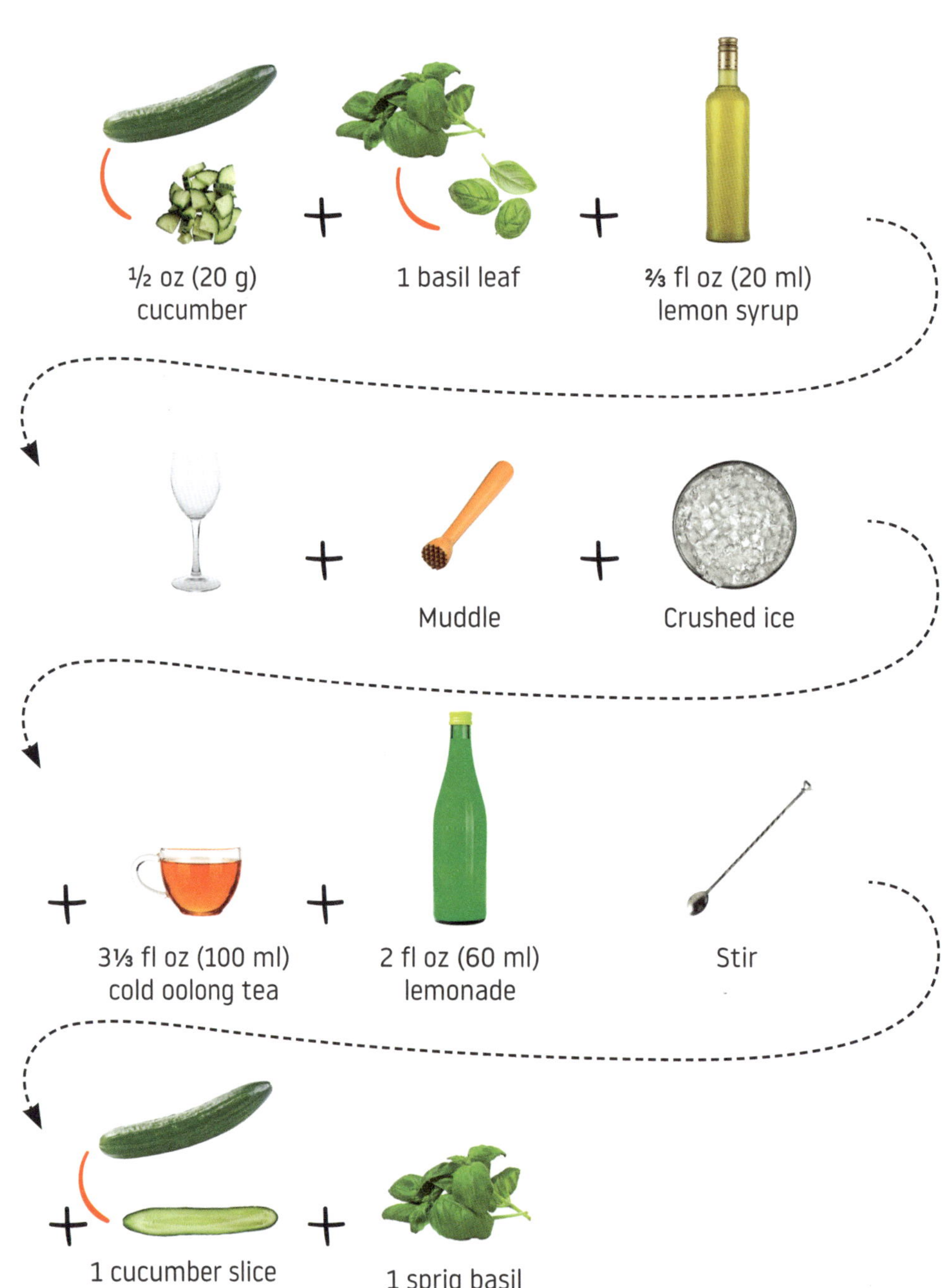
½ oz (20 g)
cucumber
1 basil leaf
⅔ fl oz (20 ml)
lemon syrup
Muddle
Crushed ice
3⅓ fl oz (100 ml)
cold oolong tea
2 fl oz (60 ml)
lemonade
Stir
1 cucumber slice
1 sprig basil

MAKES 1 GLASS
PREPARATION: 5 MINUTES

- ½ oz (20 g) cucumber, diced + 1 lengthways slice
- 1 basil leaf + 1 sprig basil
- ⅔ fl oz (20 ml) lemon syrup
- crushed ice
- 3⅓ fl oz (100 ml) cold oolong tea
- 2 fl oz (60 ml) lemonade

22 EXOTIC SOUTH AMERICA

pomegranate, guava and pineapple

¼ pomegranate
2 fl oz (60 ml) guava juice
2⅓ fl oz (70 ml) pineapple juice
Blend
3 ice cubes
1⅓ fl oz (40 ml)

Guaraná Antarctica® or V Energy Drink

1 piece pineapple

MAKES 1 GLASS
PREPARATION: 5 MINUTES

- ¼ pomegranate, diced
- 2 fl oz (60 ml) guava juice
- 2⅓ fl oz (70 ml) pineapple juice
- 3 ice cubes
- 1⅓ fl oz (40 ml) Guaraná Antarctica® or V Energy Drink
- 1 piece pineapple

23 CIAO CHICHI

elderflower, grape and apple

Crushed ice
½ lime, juiced
⅓ fl oz (10 ml) elderflower syrup
3⅓ fl oz (100 ml) white grape juice
3⅓ fl oz (100 ml) clear apple juice
½ egg white
Shake vigorously
Strain
1 dried lemon slice

MAKES 1 GLASS
PREPARATION: 5 MINUTES

- crushed ice
- ½ lime, juiced
- ⅓ fl oz (10 ml) elderflower syrup
- 3⅓ fl oz (100 ml) white grape juice
- 3⅓ fl oz (100 ml) clear apple juice
- ½ egg white (or ⅔ fl oz/20 ml aquafaba for a vegan mocktail)
- 1 dried lemon slice (optional)

24 MY LITTLE GARDEN

orange, apple and grape

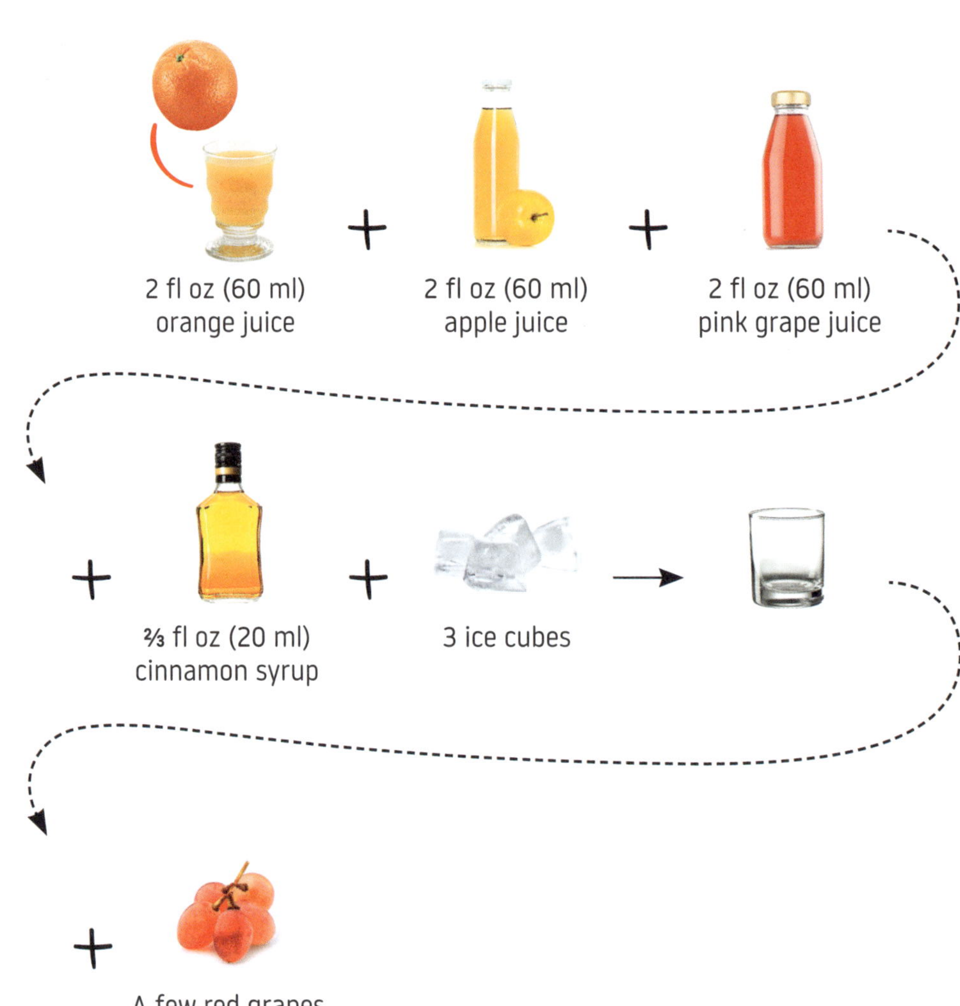
2 fl oz (60 ml)
orange juice
2 fl oz (60 ml)
apple juice
2 fl oz (60 ml)
pink grape juice
⅔ fl oz (20 ml)
cinnamon syrup
3 ice cubes
A few red grapes

MAKES 1 GLASS
PREPARATION: 5 MINUTES

- 2 fl oz (60 ml) orange juice
- 2 fl oz (60 ml) apple juice
- 2 fl oz (60 ml) pink grape juice
- ⅔ fl oz (20 ml) cinnamon syrup
- 3 ice cubes
- a few red grapes

25 ROSY GLOW

pineapple and strawberry

4 fl oz (120 ml)
pineapple juice
2½ fl oz (80 ml)
strawberry juice
⅔ fl oz (20 ml)
rose floral water
⅓ fl oz (10 ml)
blackberry syrup
4 ice cubes
Shake vigorously
3 blackberries
1 cocktail pick

MAKES 1 GLASS
PREPARATION: 5 MINUTES

- 4 fl oz (120 ml) pineapple juice
- 2½ fl oz (80 ml) strawberry juice
- ⅔ fl oz (20 ml) rose floral water
- ⅓ fl oz (10 ml) blackberry syrup
- 4 ice cubes
- 3 blackberries

26 VISIONARY

strawberry, raspberry and watermelon

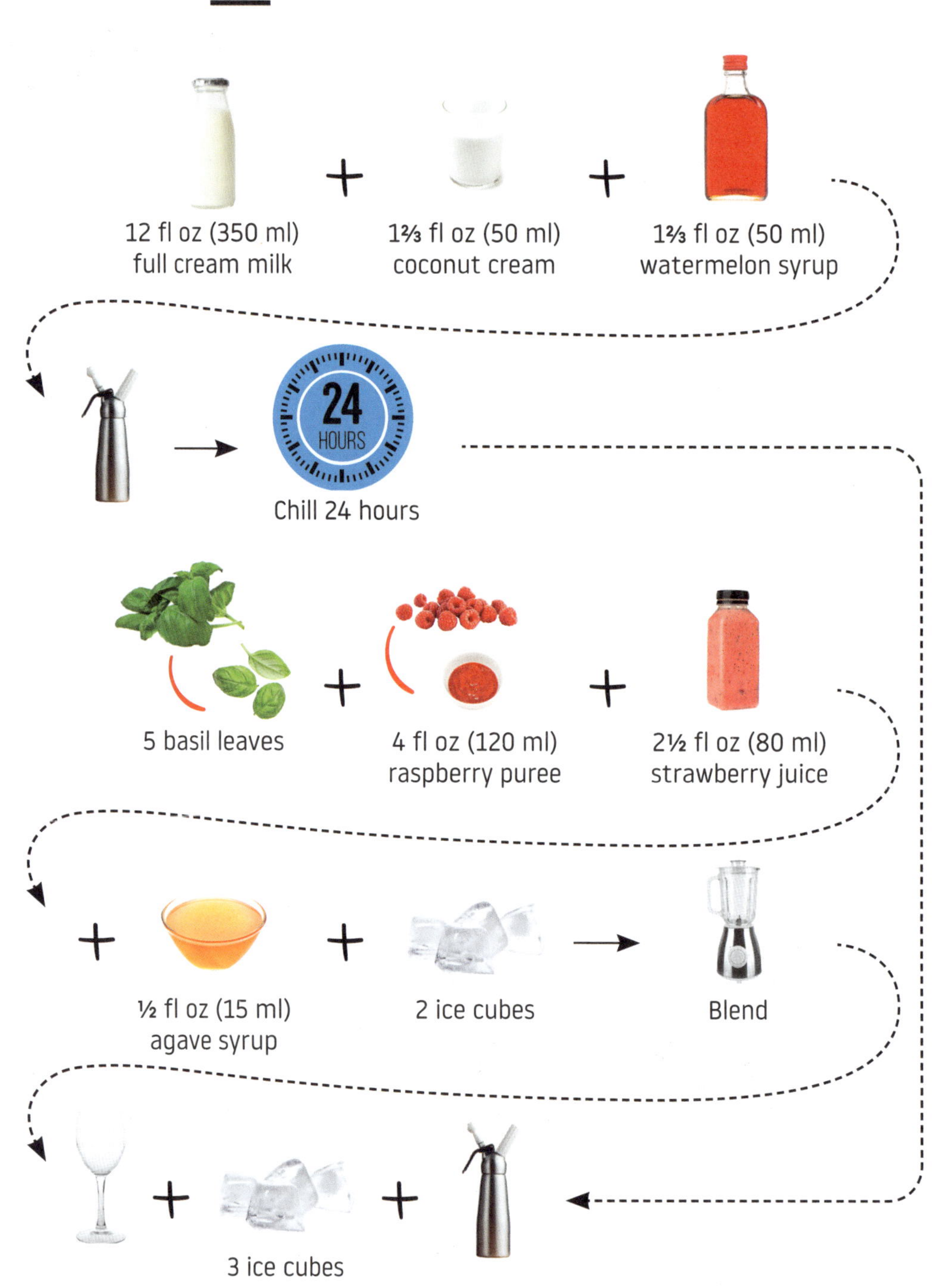
12 fl oz (350 ml)
full cream milk
+
1⅔ fl oz (50 ml)
coconut cream
+
1⅔ fl oz (50 ml)
watermelon syrup
24
HOURS
Chill 24 hours
5 basil leaves
+
4 fl oz (120 ml)
raspberry puree
+
2½ fl oz (80 ml)
strawberry juice
+
½ fl oz (15 ml)
agave syrup
+
2 ice cubes
Blend
+
3 ice cubes
+

MAKES 1 GLASS
PREPARATION: 5 MINUTES
CHILLING: 24 HOURS

- 12 fl oz (350 ml) full cream milk
- 1⅔ fl oz (50 ml) coconut cream
- 1⅔ fl oz (50 ml) watermelon syrup
- 5 basil leaves
- 4 fl oz (120 ml) raspberry puree
- 2½ fl oz (80 ml) strawberry juice
- ½ fl oz (15 ml) agave syrup
- 5 ice cubes

27 LOVE MILK

coconut, mandarin and soy

1⅓ fl oz (40 ml)
vanilla soy milk
1⅓ fl oz (40 ml)
mandarin juice
1⅓ fl oz (40 ml)
coconut water
Stir
1 vanilla pod

MAKES 1 GLASS
PREPARATION: 5 MINUTES

- 1⅓ fl oz (40 ml) vanilla soy milk
- 1⅓ fl oz (40 ml) mandarin juice
- 1⅓ fl oz (40 ml) coconut water
- 1 vanilla pod (optional)

28 EXOTIC LIPSTICK

pomegranate, vanilla and cranberry

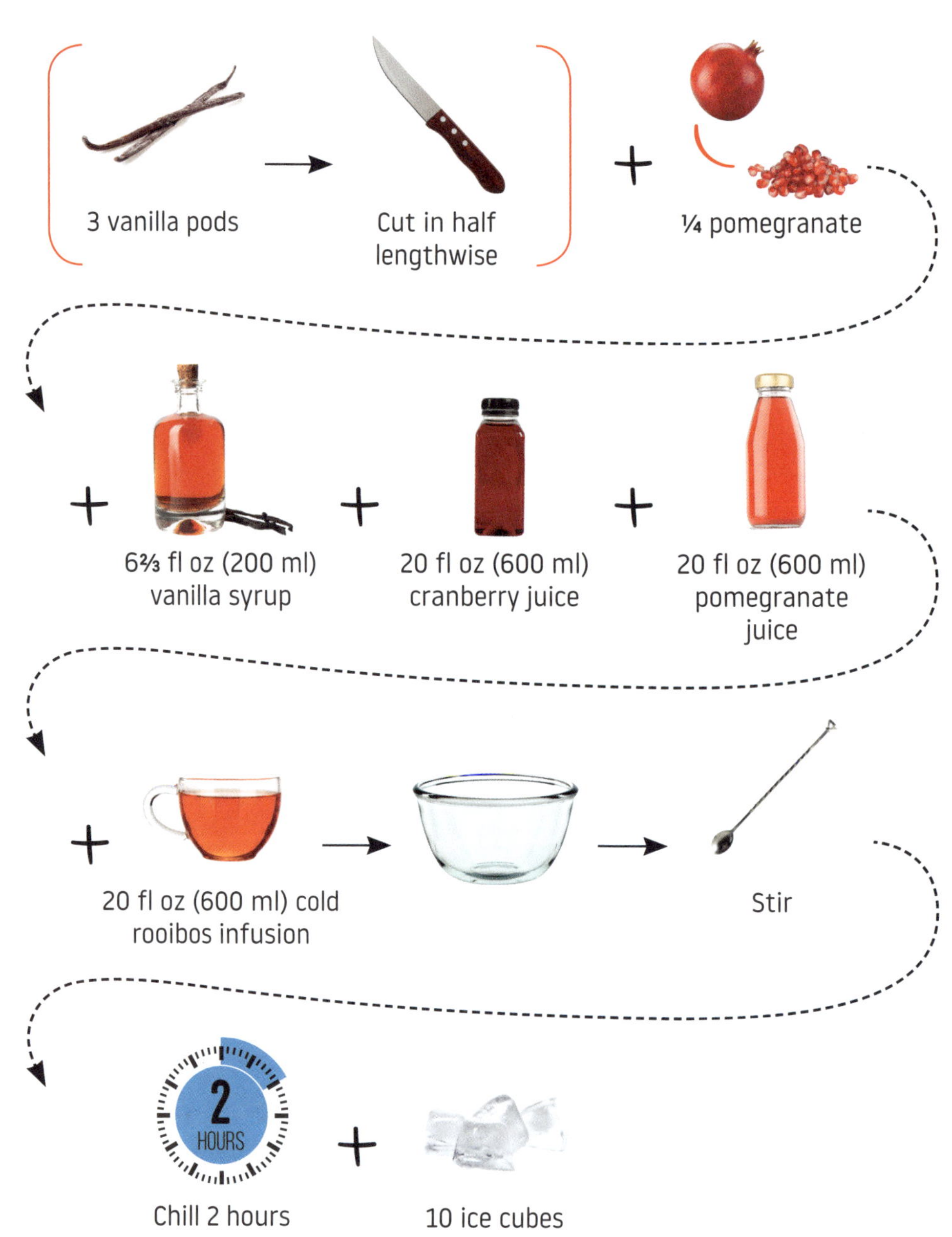

3 vanilla pods
Cut in half lengthwise
¼ pomegranate
6⅔ fl oz (200 ml) vanilla syrup
20 fl oz (600 ml) cranberry juice
20 fl oz (600 ml) pomegranate juice
20 fl oz (600 ml) cold rooibos infusion
Stir
2 HOURS
Chill 2 hours
10 ice cubes

MAKES 68 FL OZ (2 LITRES)
PREPARATION: 10 MINUTES
CHILLING: 2 HOURS

- 3 vanilla pods
- ¼ pomegranate, seeded and diced
- 6⅔ fl oz (200 ml) vanilla syrup
- 20 fl oz (600 ml) cranberry juice
- 20 fl oz (600 ml) pomegranate juice
- 20 fl oz (600 ml) cold rooibos infusion
- 10 ice cubes

29 GORGEOUS

strawberry, lemongrass and clementine

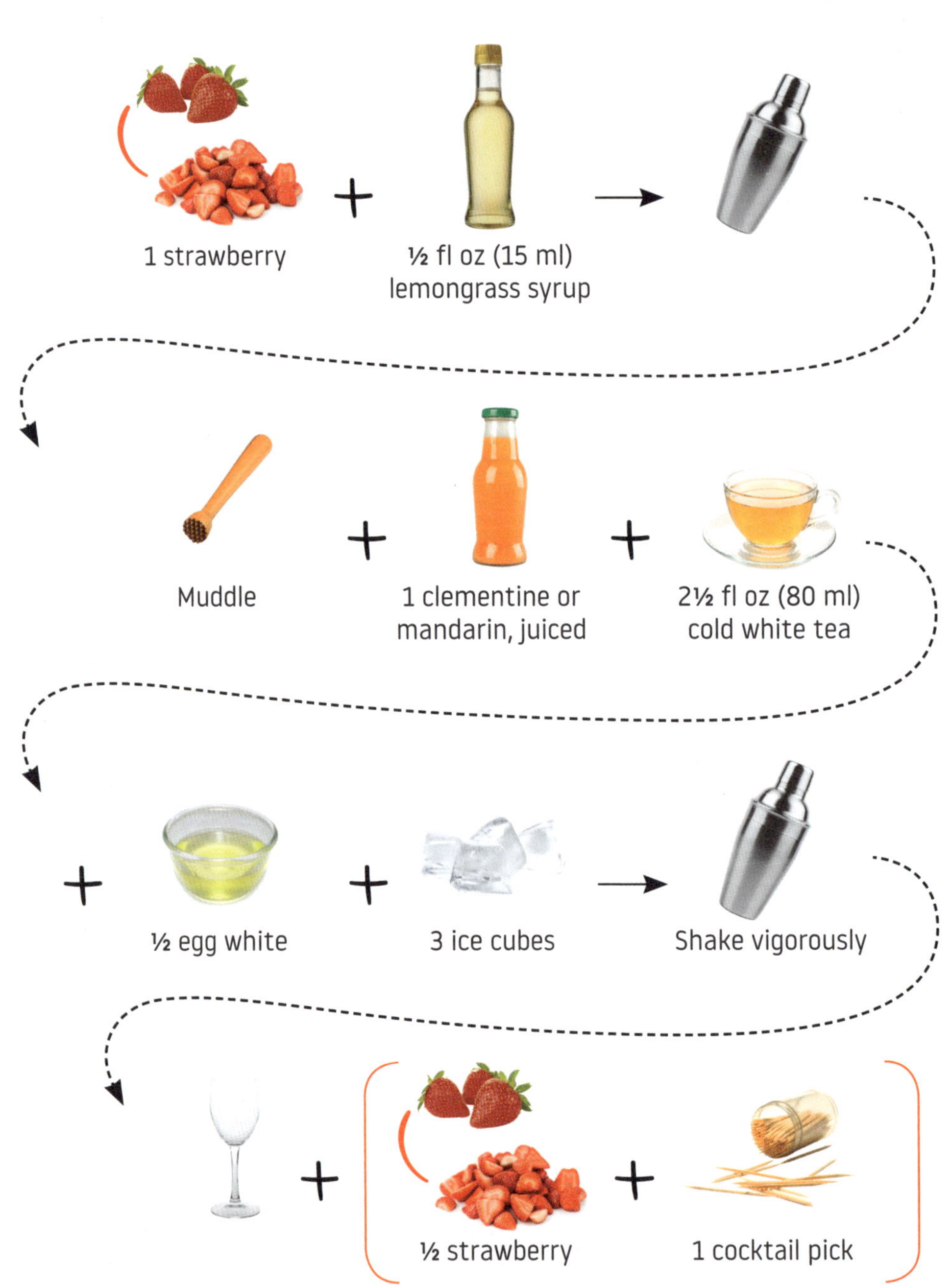
1 strawberry
½ fl oz (15 ml) lemongrass syrup
Muddle
1 clementine or mandarin, juiced
2½ fl oz (80 ml) cold white tea
½ egg white
3 ice cubes
Shake vigorously
½ strawberry
1 cocktail pick

MAKES 1 GLASS
PREPARATION: 5 MINUTES

- 1½ strawberries, sliced
- 15 ml lemongrass syrup
- 1 clementine or mandarin
- 80 ml cold white tea
- ½ egg white (or ⅔ fl oz/20 ml aquafaba for a vegan mocktail)
- 3 ice cubes

30 VEGEJITO

kiwifruit, cucumber, apple and mint

1 kiwifruit

+

½ cucumber

+

1 Granny Smith apple

+

½ celery stick

+

1 stalk lemongrass

+

1 bunch mint

+

6⅔ fl oz (200 ml) lime juice

+

SUCRE
DE CANNE

5 fl oz (150 ml) cane sugar syrup

+

Ice cubes

→

→

Stir

+

25⅓ fl oz (750 ml) fresh apple juice

5
MINUTES

Infuse 5 minutes

→

+

1 straw

SERVES 10
PREPARATION: 15 MINUTES
INFUSING: 5 MINUTES

- 1 kiwifruit, sliced
- ½ cucumber, diced
- 1 Granny Smith apple, diced
- ½ celery stick, diced
- 1 stalk lemongrass, sliced
- 1 bunch mint, chopped
- 6⅔ fl oz (200 ml) lime juice
- 5 fl oz (150 ml) cane sugar syrup
- ice cubes
- 25⅓ fl oz (750 ml) fresh apple juice

31 BANANOCOCO

with vanilla ice cream

3 ice cubes
1 banana
⅓ fl oz (10 ml) ginger syrup
1⅓ fl oz (40 ml) coconut milk
3⅓ fl oz (100 ml) coconut water
1 scoop vanilla ice cream
Blend
1 straw

23oz MAX 650ml
20
500
16
400
12
300
8
200
4
100

MAKES 1 GLASS
PREPARATION: 5 MINUTES

- 3 ice cubes
- 1 banana, sliced
- ⅓ fl oz (10 ml) ginger syrup
- 1⅓ fl oz (40 ml) coconut milk
- 3⅓ fl oz (100 ml) coconut water
- 1 scoop vanilla ice cream

32 VINTAGE VIBES

berries and hibiscus

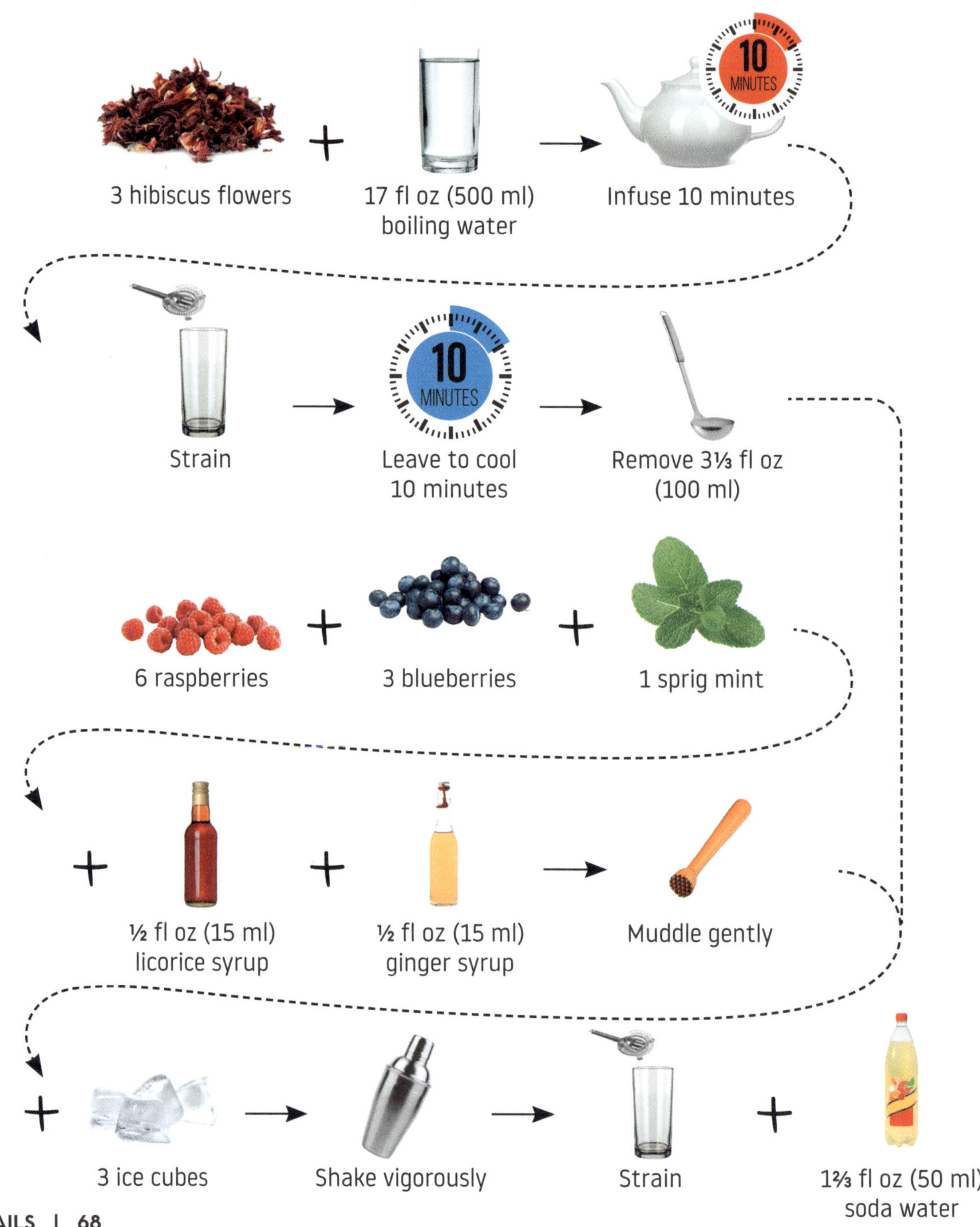

10
MINUTES
3 hibiscus flowers
17 fl oz (500 ml)
boiling water
Infuse 10 minutes
Strain
10
MINUTES
Leave to cool
10 minutes
Remove 3⅓ fl oz
(100 ml)
6 raspberries
3 blueberries
1 sprig mint
½ fl oz (15 ml)
licorice syrup
½ fl oz (15 ml)
ginger syrup
Muddle gently
3 ice cubes
Shake vigorously
Strain
1⅔ fl oz (50 ml)
soda water

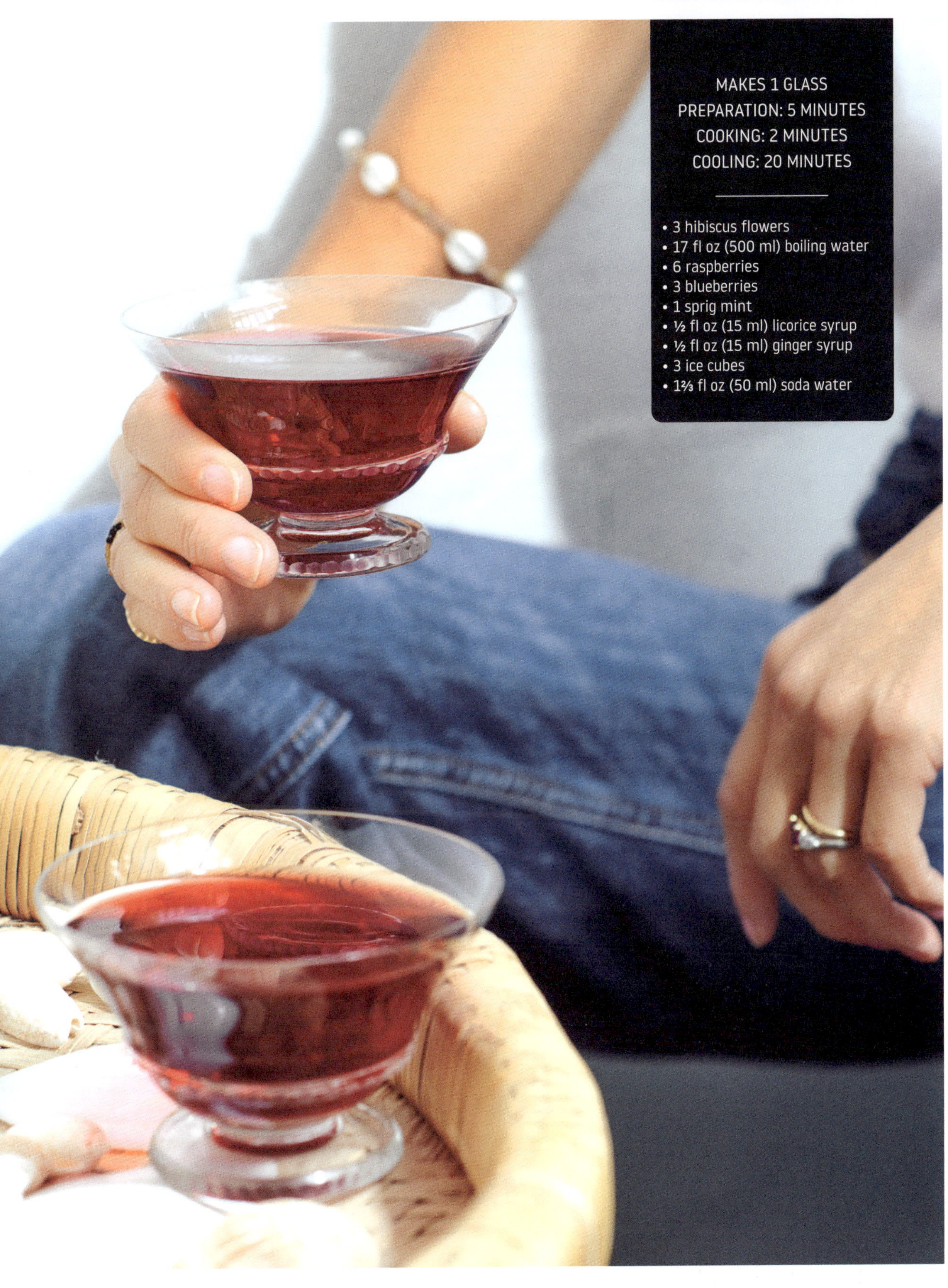

MAKES 1 GLASS
PREPARATION: 5 MINUTES
COOKING: 2 MINUTES
COOLING: 20 MINUTES

- 3 hibiscus flowers
- 17 fl oz (500 ml) boiling water
- 6 raspberries
- 3 blueberries
- 1 sprig mint
- ½ fl oz (15 ml) licorice syrup
- ½ fl oz (15 ml) ginger syrup
- 3 ice cubes
- 1⅔ fl oz (50 ml) soda water

33 MR. FRESH

cucumber, verbena and apple

¼ cucumber
½ lime, juiced
SUCRE DE CANNE
⅔ fl oz (20 ml) cane sugar syrup
3 ice cubes
3⅓ fl oz (100 ml) cold lemongrass verbena infusion
3⅓ fl oz (100 ml) apple juice
Stir
1 cucumber slice
1 lime slice

MAKES 1 GLASS
PREPARATION: 5 MINUTES

- ¼ cucumber, diced + 1 slice
- ½ lime, juiced + 1 slice
- ⅔ fl oz (20 ml) cane sugar syrup
- 3 ice cubes
- 3⅓ fl oz (100 ml) cold lemongrass verbena infusion
- 3⅓ fl oz (100 ml) apple juice

34 BLISS

berries and yogurt

2½ fl oz (80 ml)
raspberry juice
2½ fl oz (80 ml)
strawberry juice
⅔ fl oz (20 ml)
blackcurrant syrup
½ small tub
natural yogurt
4 ice cubes
Blend

MAKES 1 GLASS
PREPARATION: 5 MINUTES

- 2½ fl oz (80 ml) raspberry juice
- 2½ fl oz (80 ml) strawberry juice
- ⅔ fl oz (20 ml) blackcurrant syrup
- ½ small tub natural yogurt
- 4 ice cubes

35 SUMMER IDEA

grapefruit, rosemary and cucumber

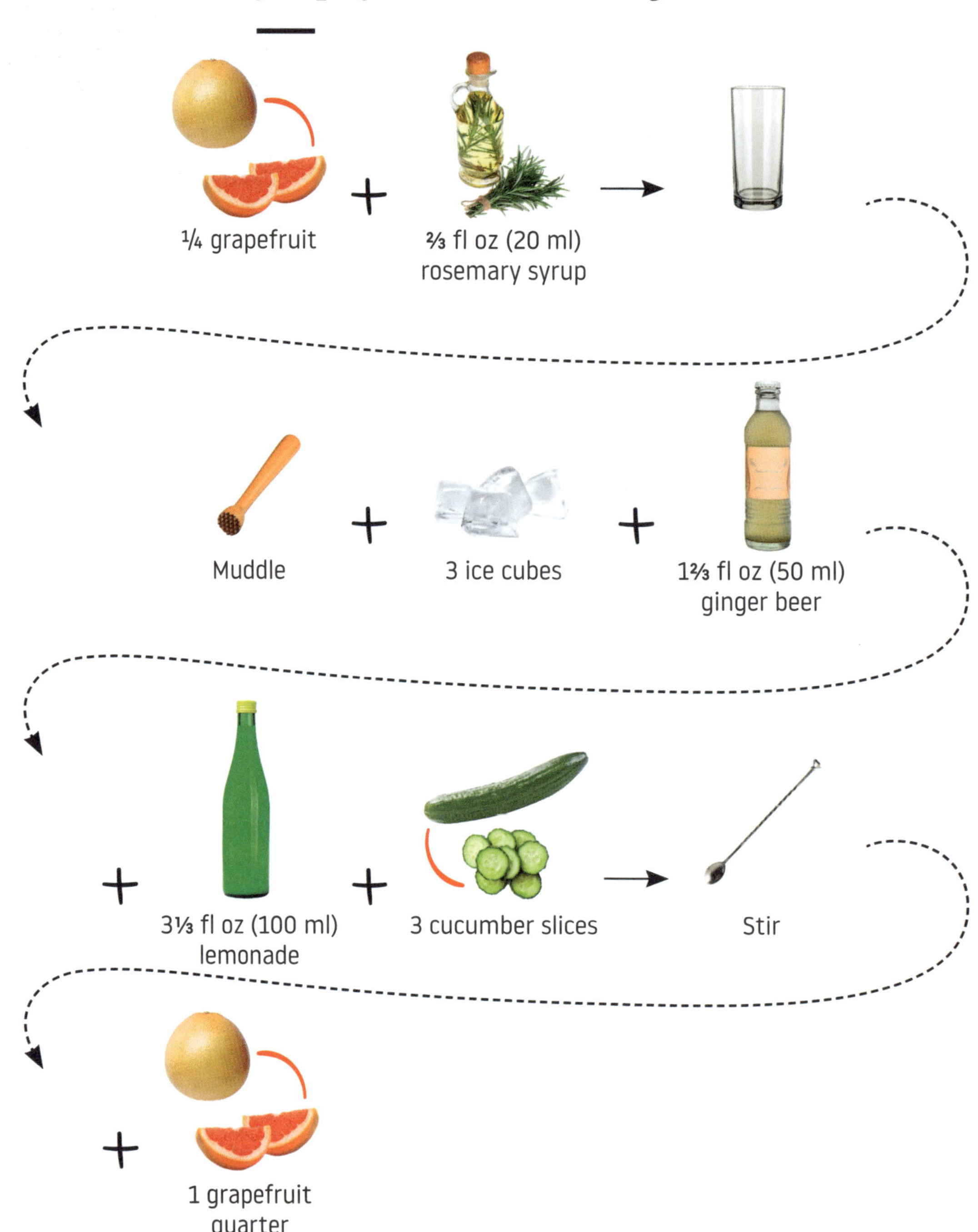
¼ grapefruit
⅔ fl oz (20 ml) rosemary syrup
Muddle
3 ice cubes
1⅔ fl oz (50 ml) ginger beer
3⅓ fl oz (100 ml) lemonade
3 cucumber slices
Stir
1 grapefruit quarter

MAKES 1 GLASS
PREPARATION: 5 MINUTES

- ¼ grapefruit, cut in half slices + 1 grapefruit quarter
- ⅔ fl oz (20 ml) rosemary syrup
- 3 ice cubes
- 1⅔ fl oz (50 ml) ginger beer
- 3⅓ fl oz (100 ml) lemonade
- 3 cucumber slices

36 ITALIAN DETOX

pineapple, watermelon and tomato

3⅓ fl oz (100 ml) pineapple juice
+
3½ oz (100 g) watermelon flesh
+
1 truss cherry tomatoes
Blend
+
Crushed ice
+
2 watermelon pieces
+
½ cherry tomato
+
1 straw

MAKES 1 GLASS
PREPARATION: 5 MINUTES

- 3⅓ fl oz (100 ml) pineapple juice
- 3½ oz (100 g) watermelon flesh, diced + 2 pieces
- 1 truss cherry tomatoes + ½ cherry tomato
- crushed ice

37 BORN TO BE RED

capsicum, strawberry and cranberry

¼ red capsicum
5 mint leaves
3⅓ fl oz (100 ml) strawberry juice
2½ fl oz (80 ml) cranberry juice
1 dash Tabasco®
Ice cubes
20 SECONDS
Blend 20 seconds
1 bunch redcurrants
1 mint leaf

MAKES 1 GLASS
PREPARATION: 5 MINUTES

- ¼ red capsicum, diced
- 6 mint leaves
- 3⅓ fl oz (100 ml) strawberry juice
- 2½ fl oz (80 ml) cranberry juice
- 1 dash Tabasco®
- ice cubes
- 1 bunch redcurrants

38 TROPICANA

orange, mango and rosemary

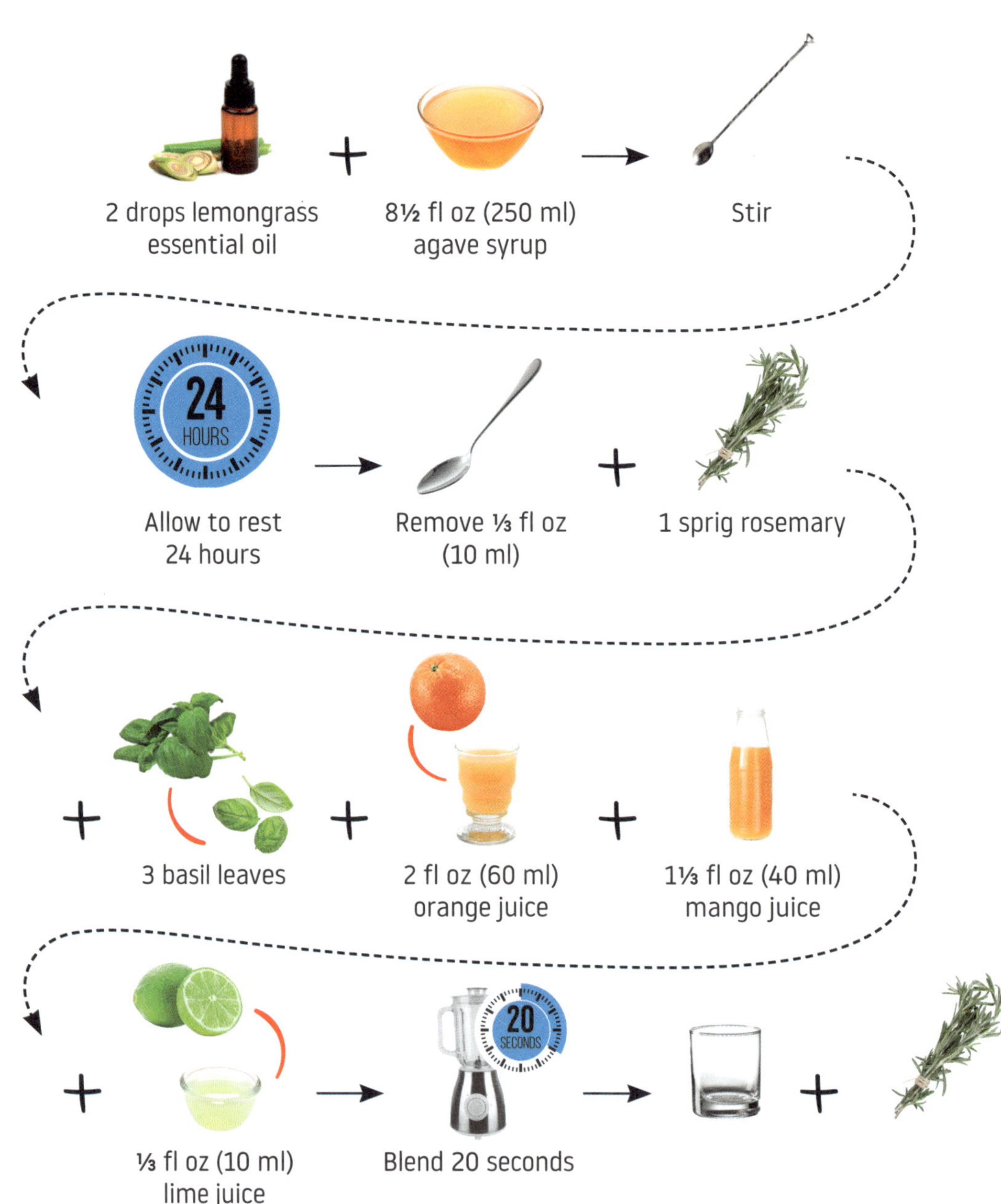

2 drops lemongrass essential oil
8½ fl oz (250 ml) agave syrup
Stir
24
HOURS
Allow to rest 24 hours
Remove ⅓ fl oz (10 ml)
1 sprig rosemary
3 basil leaves
2 fl oz (60 ml) orange juice
1⅓ fl oz (40 ml) mango juice
⅓ fl oz (10 ml) lime juice
20
SECONDS
Blend 20 seconds

MAKES 1 GLASS
PREPARATION: 5 MINUTES
RESTING: 24 HOURS

- 2 drops lemongrass essential oil
- 8½ fl oz (250 ml) agave syrup
- 2 sprigs rosemary
- 3 basil leaves
- 2 fl oz (60 ml) orange juice
- 1⅓ fl oz (40 ml) mango juice
- ⅓ fl oz (10 ml) lime juice

39 CANDIDE

iced tea and lime

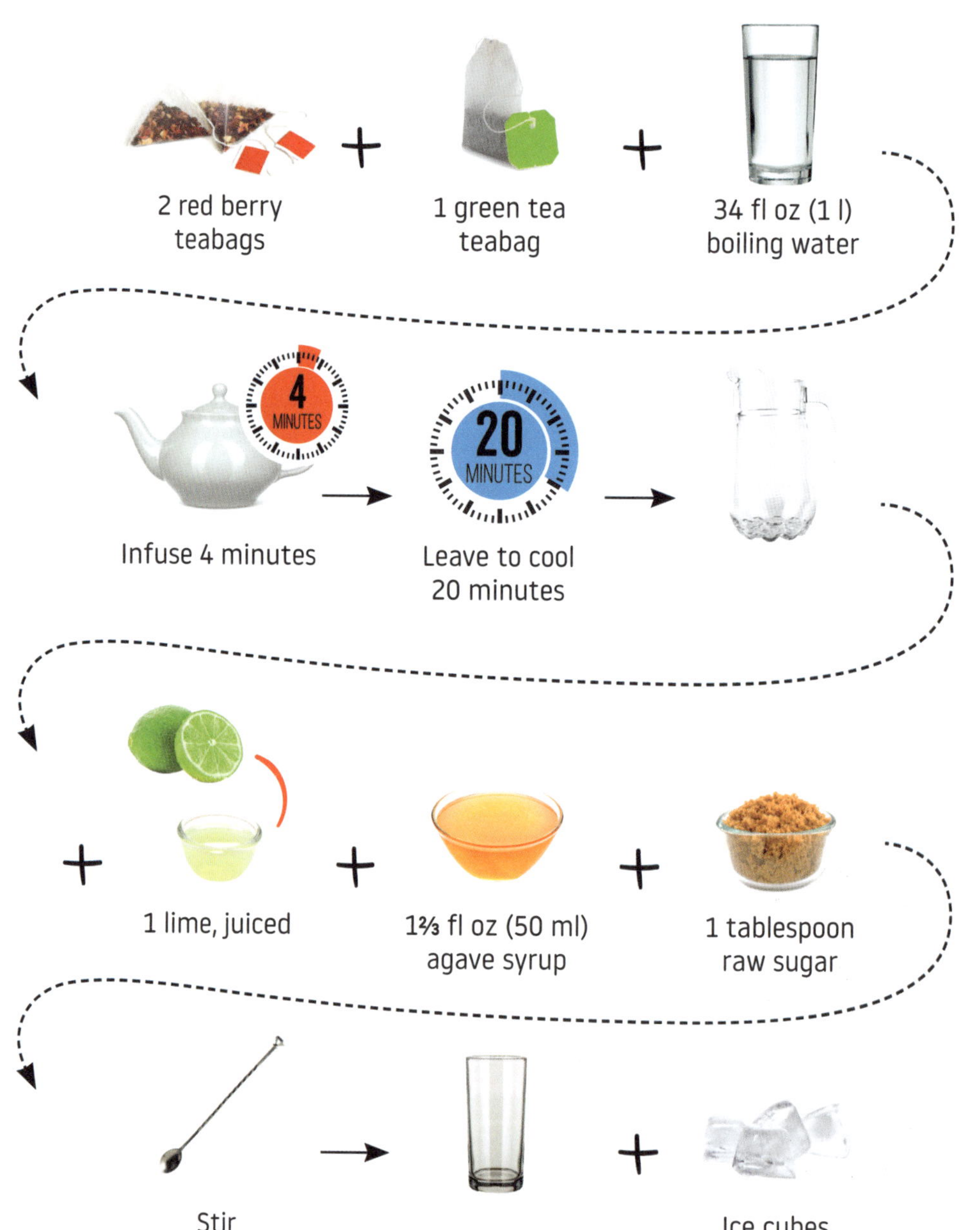
2 red berry teabags
1 green tea teabag
34 fl oz (1 l) boiling water
4 MINUTES
Infuse 4 minutes
20 MINUTES
Leave to cool 20 minutes
1 lime, juiced
1⅔ fl oz (50 ml) agave syrup
1 tablespoon raw sugar
Stir
Ice cubes

MAKES 34 FL OZ (1 LITRE)
PREPARATION: 10 MINUTES
INFUSING: 4 MINUTES
COOLING: 20 MINUTES

- 2 red berry teabags
- 1 green tea teabag
- 34 fl oz (1 l) boiling water
- 1 lime, juiced
- 1⅔ fl oz (50 ml) agave syrup
- 1 tablespoon raw sugar
- ice cubes

40 SUMMER KISS

melon, strawberry and cucumber

5⅓ oz (150 g)
strawberries
Cut in half
15 ice cubes
1 rockmelon
½ cucumber
Blend
34 fl oz (1 l)
sparkling water

MAKES 51 FL OZ (1.5 LITRES)
PREPARATION: 10 MINUTES

- 5⅓ oz (150 g) strawberries, halved
- 15 ice cubes
- 1 rockmelon, diced
- ½ cucumber, diced
- 34 fl oz (1 l) sparkling water

41 KIWIFRUIT FRESH

apple, grape and pineapple

½ kiwifruit
1 fl oz (30 ml) green apple juice
1 fl oz (30 ml) white grape juice
1 fl oz (30 ml) pineapple juice
Blend
3 ice cubes

MAKES 1 GLASS
PREPARATION: 5 MINUTES

- ½ kiwifruit, sliced
- 1 fl oz (30 ml) green apple juice
- 1 fl oz (30 ml) white grape juice
- 1 fl oz (30 ml) pineapple juice
- 3 ice cubes

42 CRISP WATERMELON *with coriander*

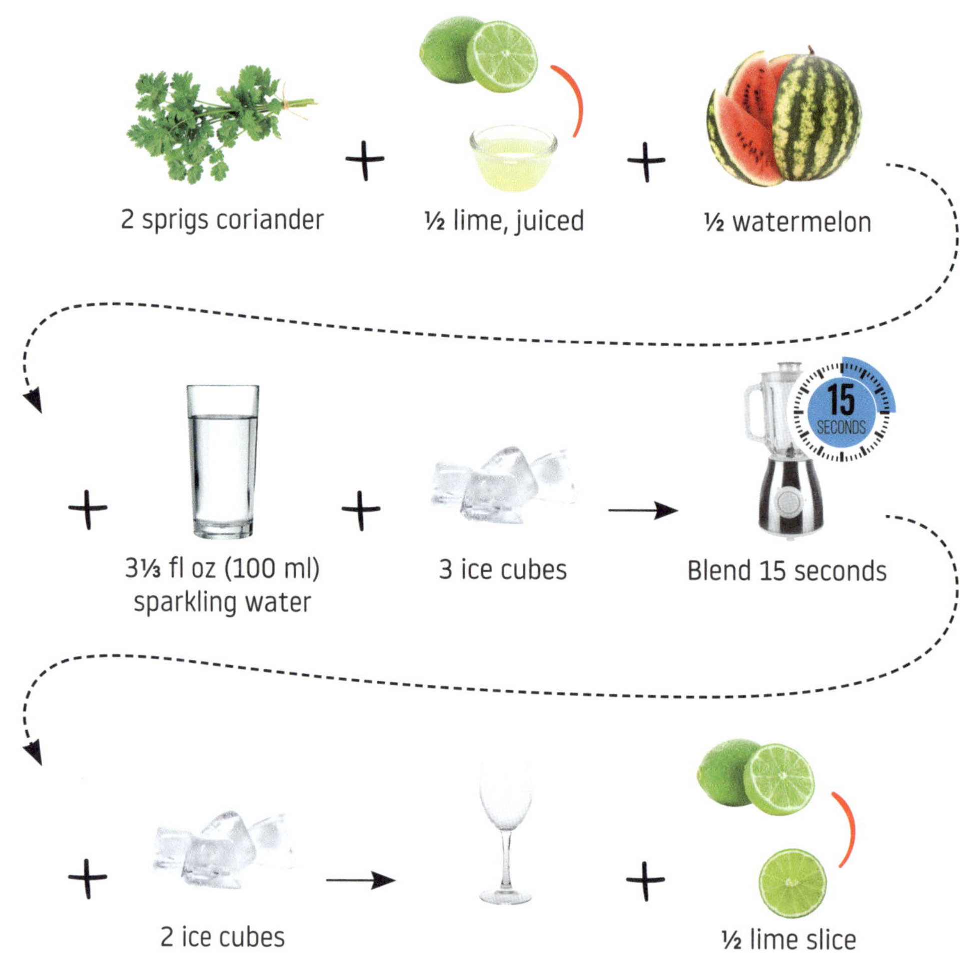

2 sprigs coriander
½ lime, juiced
½ watermelon
3⅓ fl oz (100 ml) sparkling water
3 ice cubes
15 SECONDS
Blend 15 seconds
2 ice cubes
½ lime slice

MAKES 1 GLASS
PREPARATION: 5 MINUTES

- 2 sprigs coriander
- 1 lime, juiced + ½ lime slice
- ½ watermelon, diced
- 3⅓ fl oz (100 ml) sparkling water
- 5 ice cubes

43 GOLDEN SPICE

star anise, orange and ginger

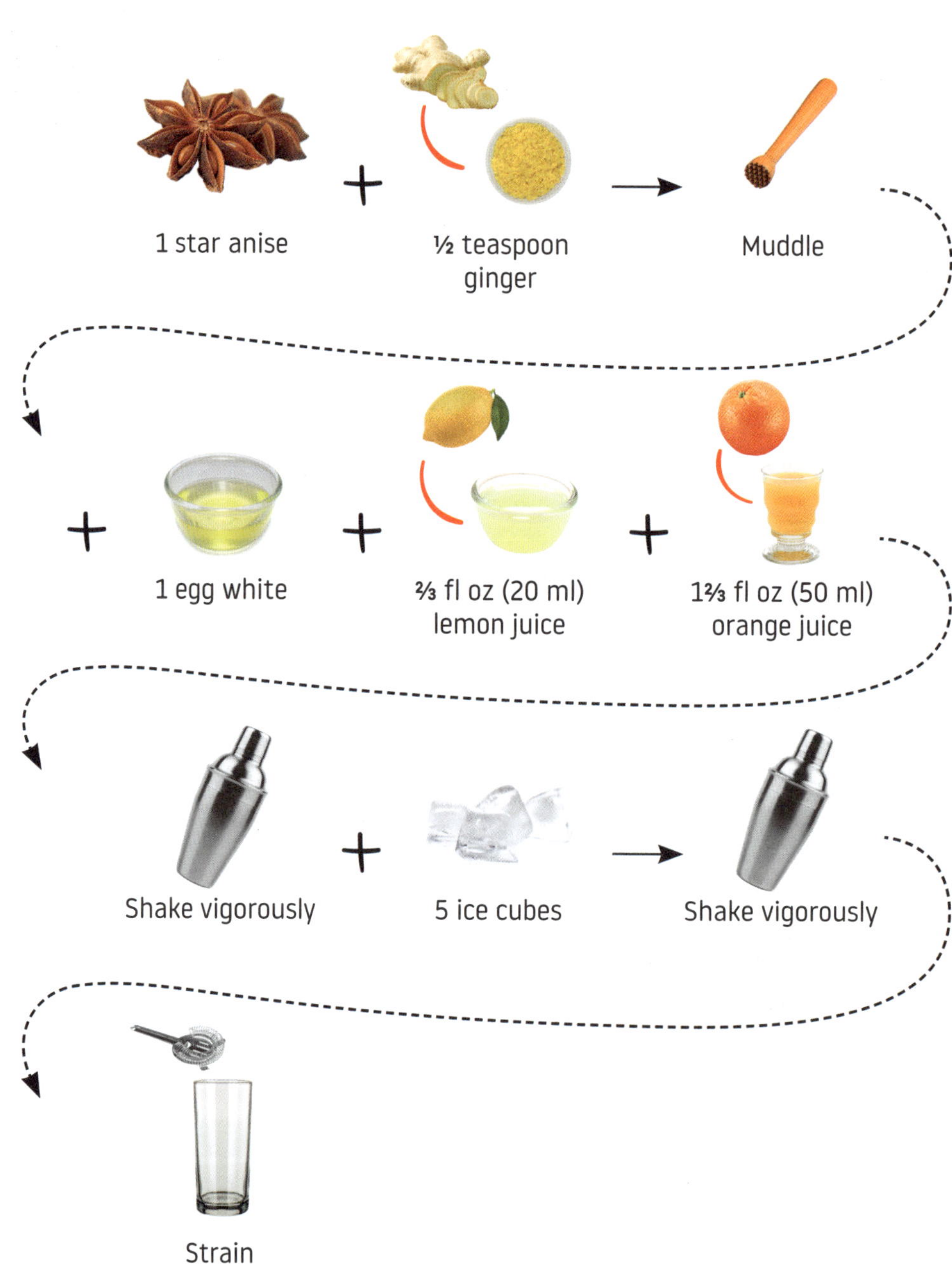

1 star anise
½ teaspoon ginger
Muddle
1 egg white
⅔ fl oz (20 ml) lemon juice
1⅔ fl oz (50 ml) orange juice
Shake vigorously
5 ice cubes
Shake vigorously
Strain

MAKES 1 GLASS
PREPARATION: 5 MINUTES

- 1 star anise
- ½ teaspoon fresh ginger
- 1 egg white
- ⅔ fl oz (20 ml) lemon juice
- 1⅔ fl oz (50 ml) orange juice
- 5 ice cubes

44 SHAKE ME

lime, kiwifruit and orange

½ lime
½ kiwifruit
1 sprig mint
Muddle
3 ice cubes
ORANGINA
1 can Orangina®
or orange soda
1 kiwifruit slice

MAKES 1 GLASS
PREPARATION: 5 MINUTES

- ½ lime, diced
- ½ kiwifruit, sliced + 1 slice
- 1 sprig mint
- 3 ice cubes
- 1 can Orangina® or orange soda

45 FLAVOR TANGO

tomato, tea and cranberry

3 cherry tomatoes
+
⅓ fl oz (10 ml) Spiced Winter Berries® cordial
→
Muddle
+
4 ice cubes
+
1 fl oz (30 ml) cold red berry tea
+
1 fl oz (30 ml) cranberry juice
→
Stir
+
⅔ fl oz (20 ml) sparkling water
+
1 bird's eye chilli

MAKES 1 GLASS
PREPARATION: 5 MINUTES

- 3 cherry tomatoes
- ⅓ fl oz (10 ml) Spiced Winter Berries® cordial or blackcurrant syrup
- 4 ice cubes
- 1 fl oz (30 ml) cold red berry tea
- 1 fl oz (30 ml) cranberry juice
- ⅔ fl oz (20 ml) sparkling water
- 1 bird's eye chilli, partially sliced vertically

46 PURPLE SHAKE

blackberry, almond and pear

4 blackberries
1 tablespoon almonds
2⅓ fl oz (70 ml) rice milk
2⅓ fl oz (70 ml) pear juice
20 SECONDS
Blend 20 seconds

MAKES 1 GLASS
PREPARATION: 5 MINUTES

- 4 blackberries
- 1 tablespoon almonds
- 2⅓ fl oz (70 ml) rice milk
- 2⅓ fl oz (70 ml) pear juice

47 SUMMER DREAM

strawberry, orange and mango

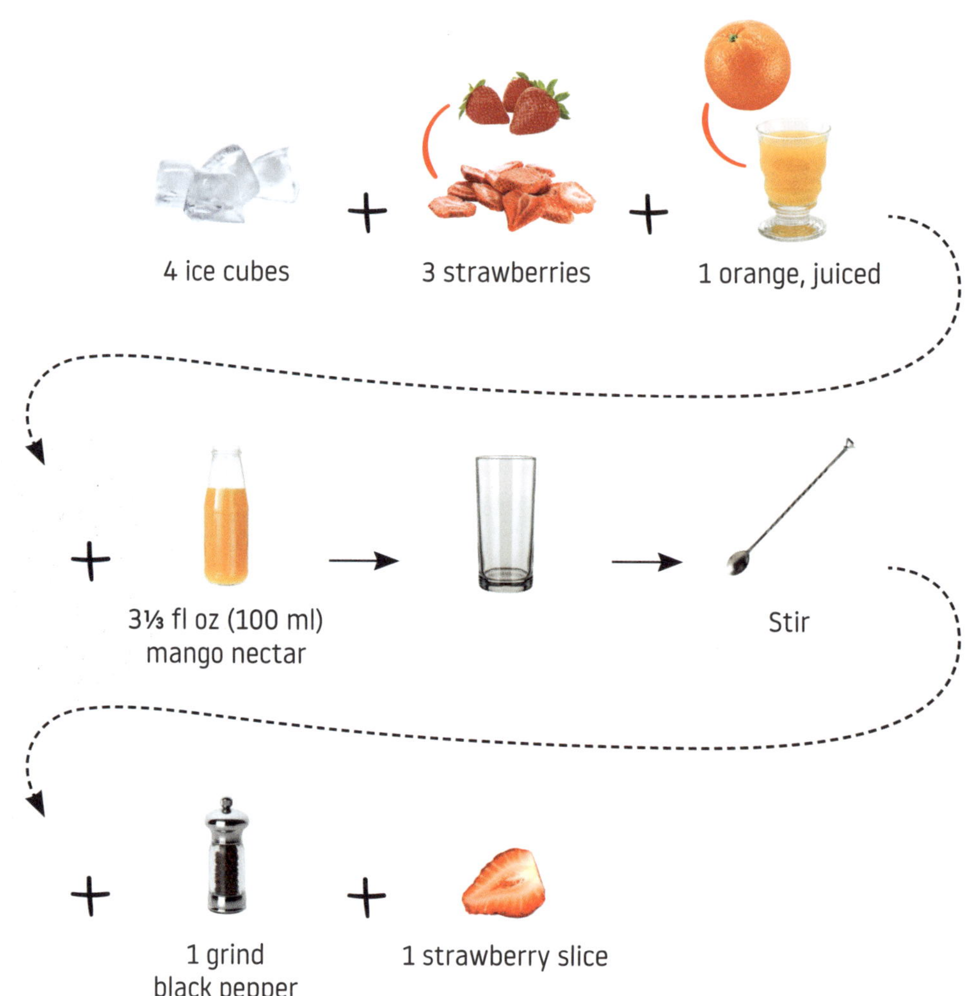

4 ice cubes
3 strawberries
1 orange, juiced
3⅓ fl oz (100 ml) mango nectar
Stir
1 grind black pepper
1 strawberry slice

MAKES 1 GLASS
PREPARATION: 5 MINUTES

- 4 ice cubes
- 3 strawberries sliced + extra for garnish
- 1 strawberry slice
- 1 orange, juiced
- 3⅓ fl oz (100 ml) mango nectar
- 1 grind black pepper

48 EXOTIC

banana, mango and vanilla

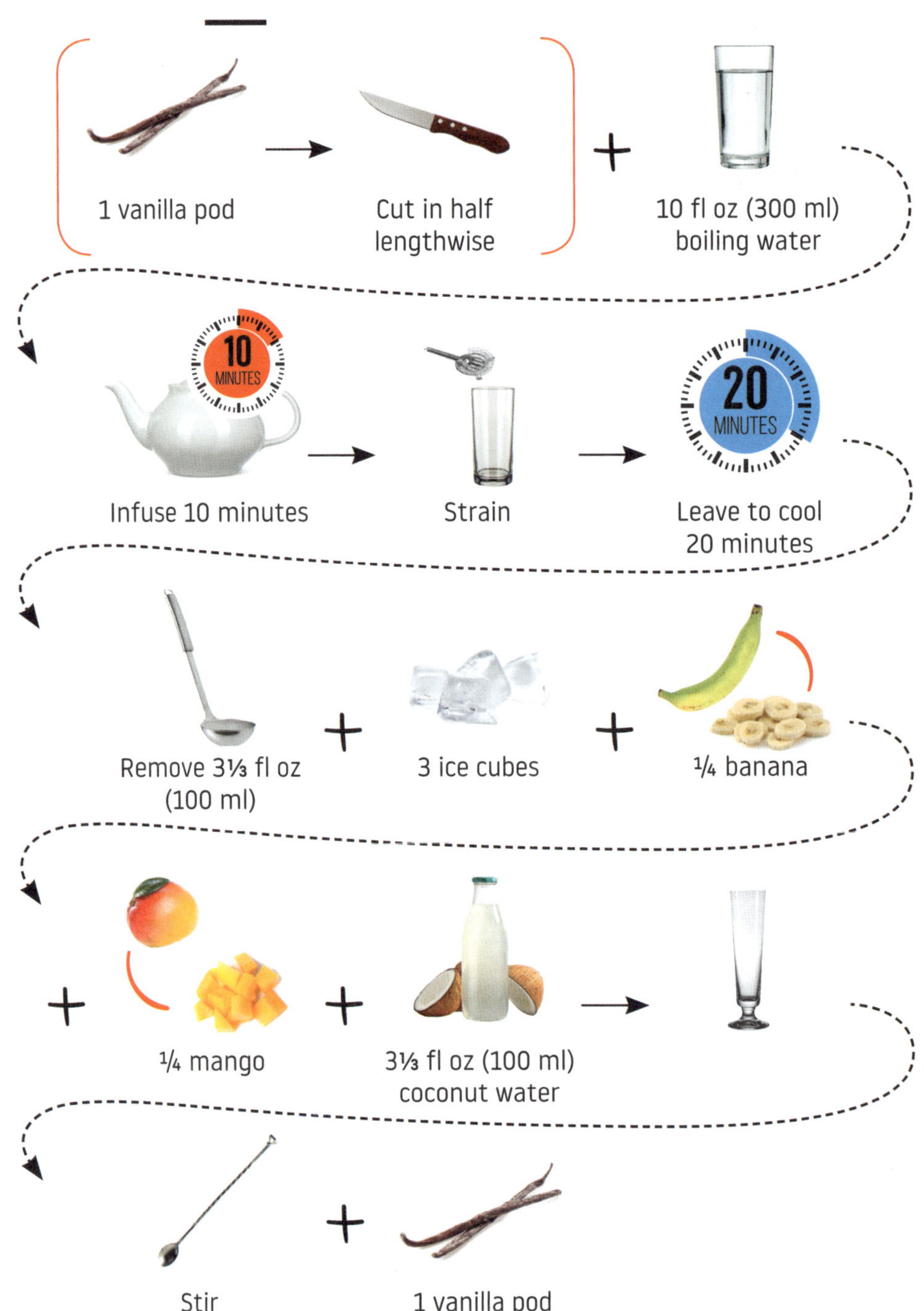
1 vanilla pod
Cut in half lengthwise
10 fl oz (300 ml) boiling water
10 MINUTES
Infuse 10 minutes
Strain
20 MINUTES
Leave to cool 20 minutes
Remove 3⅓ fl oz (100 ml)
3 ice cubes
¼ banana
¼ mango
3⅓ fl oz (100 ml) coconut water
Stir
1 vanilla pod

MAKES 1 GLASS
PREPARATION: 5 MINUTES
INFUSING: 10 MINUTES
COOLING: 20 MINUTES

- 2 vanilla pods
- 10 fl oz (300 ml) boiling water
- 3 ice cubes
- ¼ banana, sliced
- ¼ mango, diced
- 3⅓ fl oz (100 ml) coconut water

49 HOME-STYLE *lemonade*

5 MINUTES
6⅔ fl oz (200 ml) honey
6⅔ fl oz (200 ml) water
Heat 5 minutes
20 MINUTES
4 lemons, juiced
Leave to cool
44 fl oz (1.3 l) water
2 lemons
½ bunch mint
10 ice cubes
Stir

MAKES 68 FL OZ (2 LITRES)
PREPARATION: 5 MINUTES
COOKING: 5 MINUTES
COOLING: 20 MINUTES

- 6⅔ fl oz (200 ml) honey
- 6⅔ fl oz (200 ml) water
- 4 lemons, juiced + 2 lemons, sliced
- 44 fl oz (1.3 l) water
- ½ bunch mint
- 10 ice cubes

50 ORIGINAL FRESH

redcurrant and soda

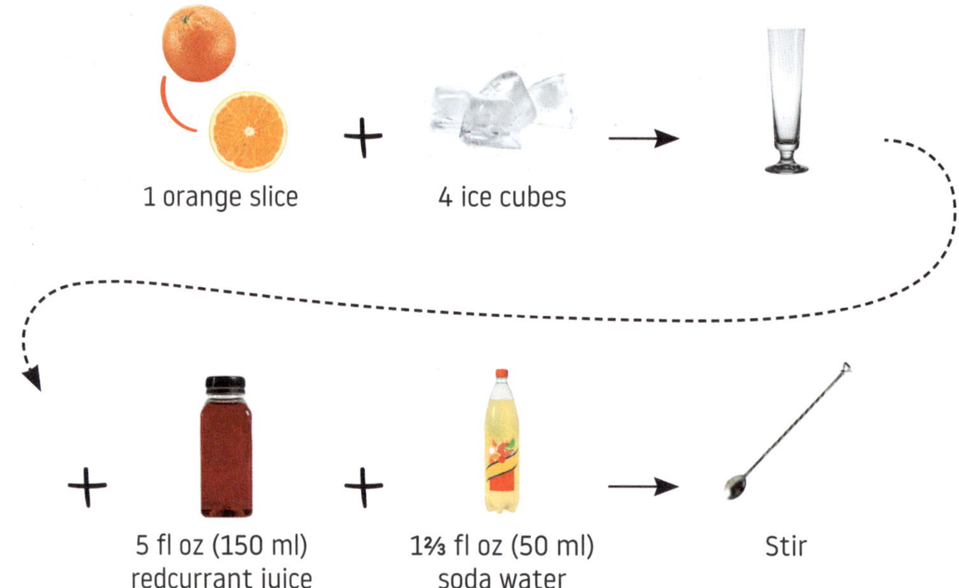
1 orange slice
4 ice cubes
5 fl oz (150 ml) redcurrant juice
1⅔ fl oz (50 ml) soda water
Stir

MAKES 1 GLASS
PREPARATION: 5 MINUTES

- 1 orange slice
- 4 ice cubes
- 5 fl oz (150 ml) redcurrant or cranberry juice
- 1⅔ fl oz (50 ml) soda water

51 LUSCIOUS LEMON

rockmelon and coriander

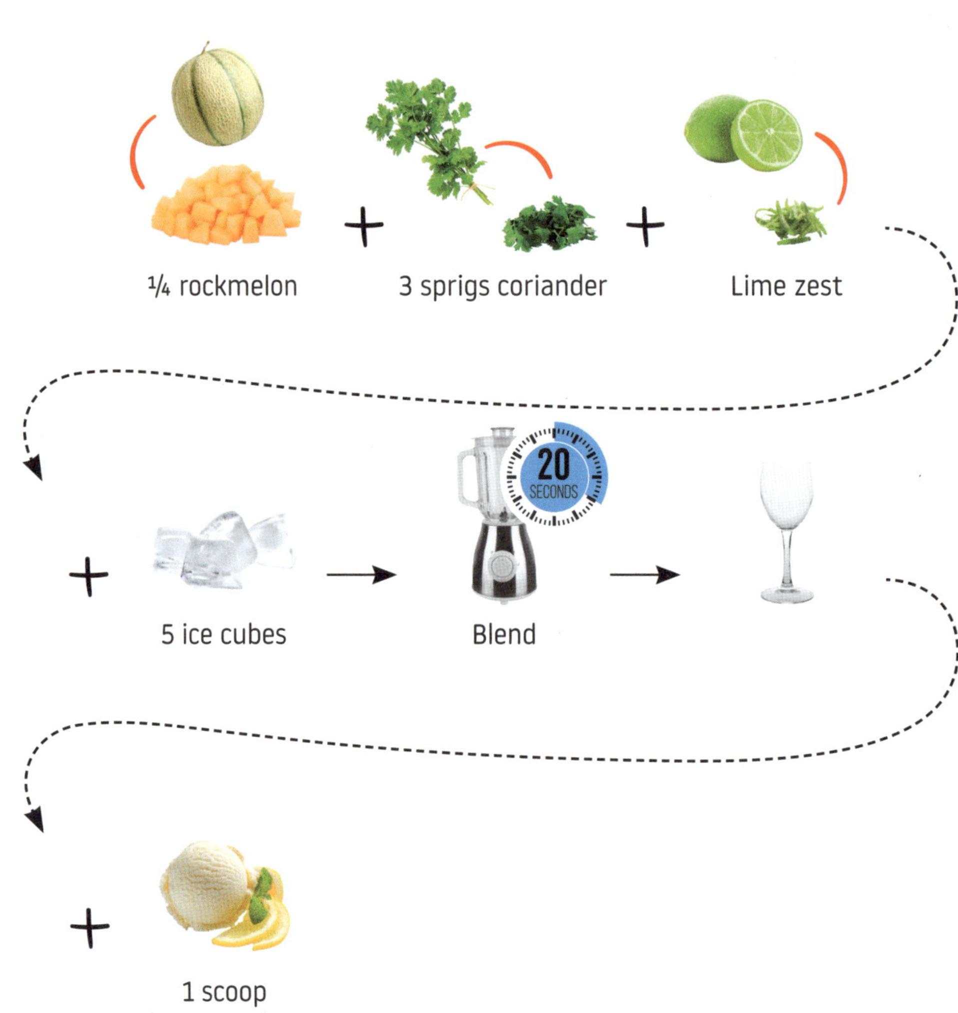

¼ rockmelon
3 sprigs coriander
Lime zest
5 ice cubes
20
SECONDS
Blend

1 scoop
lemon sorbet

MAKES 1 GLASS
PREPARATION: 5 MINUTES

- ¼ rockmelon, diced
- 3 sprigs coriander
- lime zest
- 5 ice cubes
- 1 scoop lemon sorbet

52 TART AND TANGY

mustard, grapefruit and apple

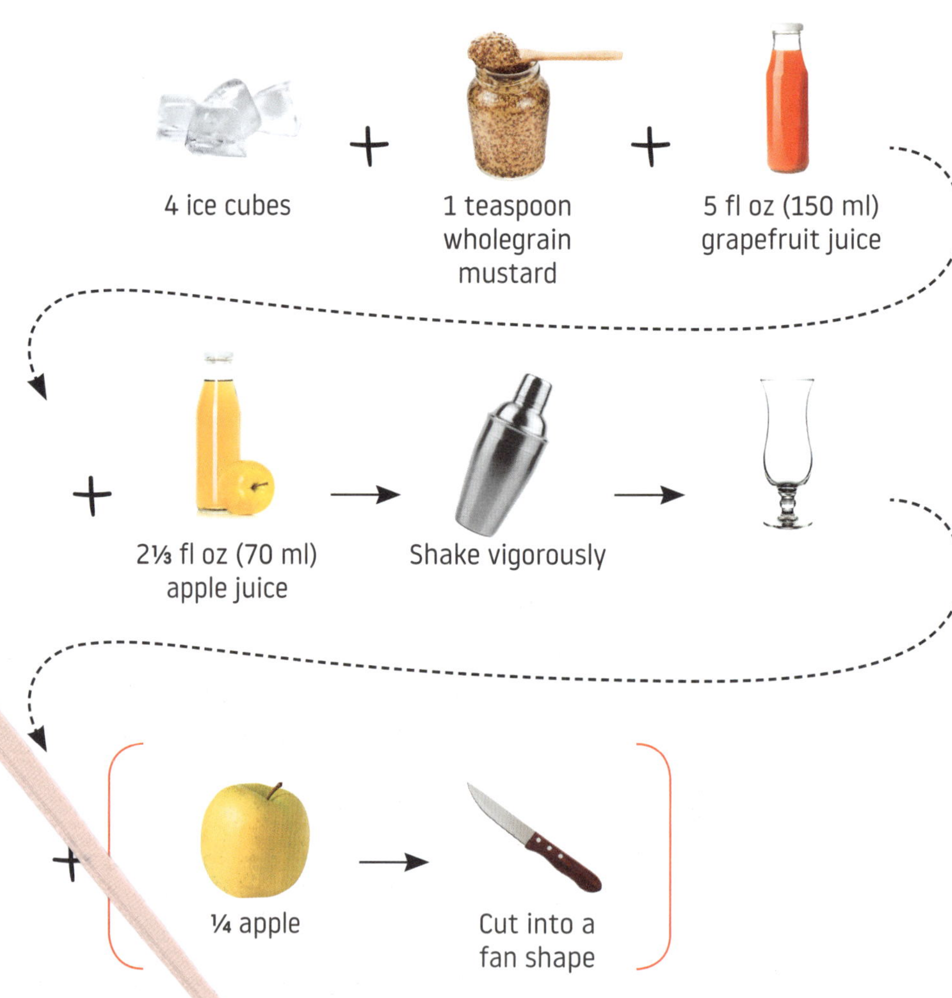

4 ice cubes
1 teaspoon wholegrain mustard
5 fl oz (150 ml) grapefruit juice
2⅓ fl oz (70 ml) apple juice
Shake vigorously
¼ apple
Cut into a fan shape

MAKES 1 GLASS
PREPARATION: 5 MINUTES

- 4 ice cubes
- 1 teaspoon wholegrain mustard
- 5 fl oz (150 ml) grapefruit juice
- 2⅓ fl oz (70 ml) apple juice
- ¼ apple, cut into a fan shape

53 THREE LITTLE BIRDS

pineapple, fig and coconut

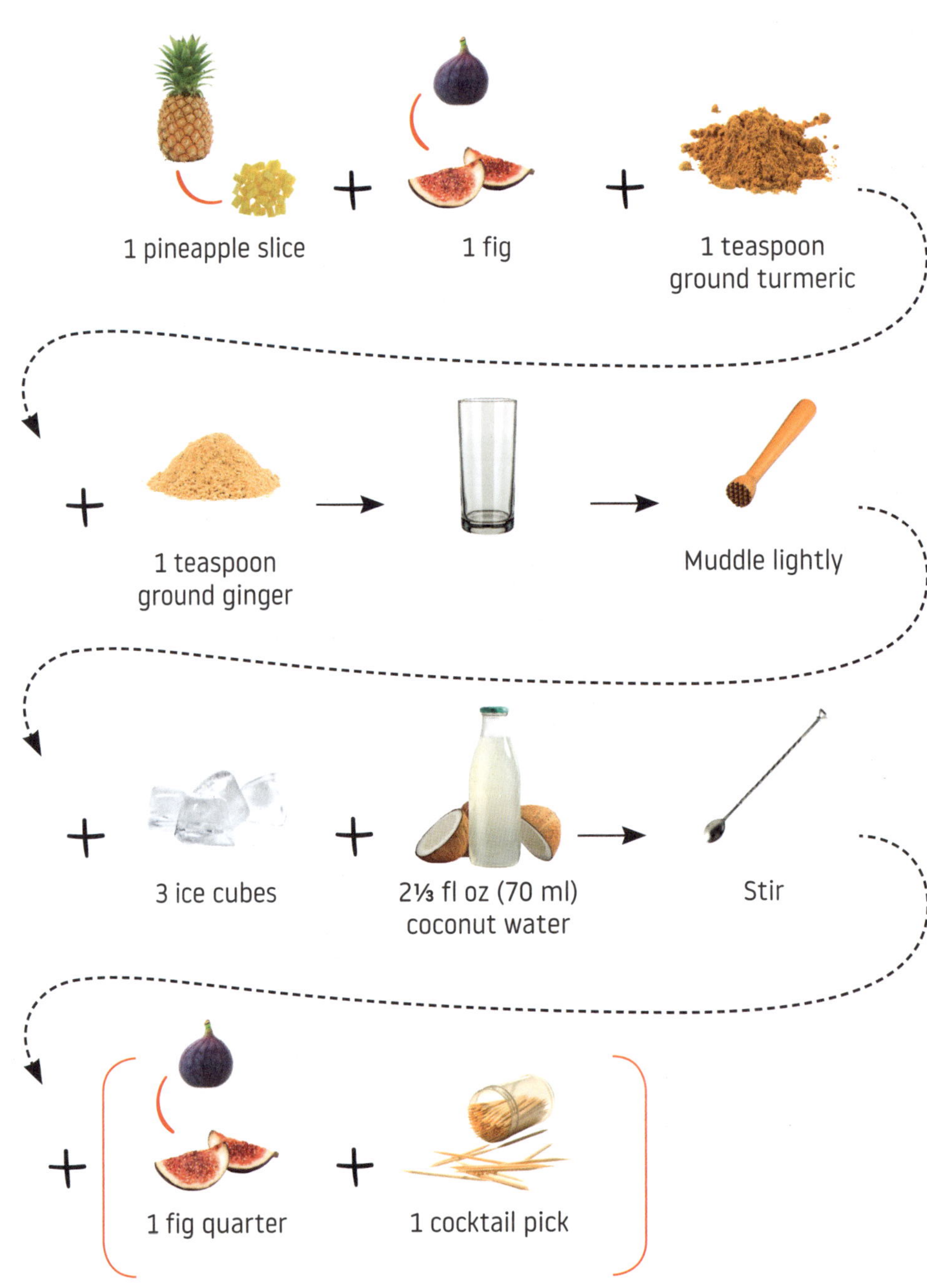
1 pineapple slice
1 fig
1 teaspoon ground turmeric
1 teaspoon ground ginger
Muddle lightly
3 ice cubes
2⅓ fl oz (70 ml) coconut water
Stir
1 fig quarter
1 cocktail pick

MAKES 1 GLASS
PREPARATION: 5 MINUTES

- 1 pineapple slice, diced
- 1 fig, quartered + 1 quarter
- 1 teaspoon ground turmeric
- 1 teaspoon ground ginger
- 3 ice cubes
- 2⅓ fl oz (70 ml) coconut water

54 NICE AND PEACHY

with cherries and apricots

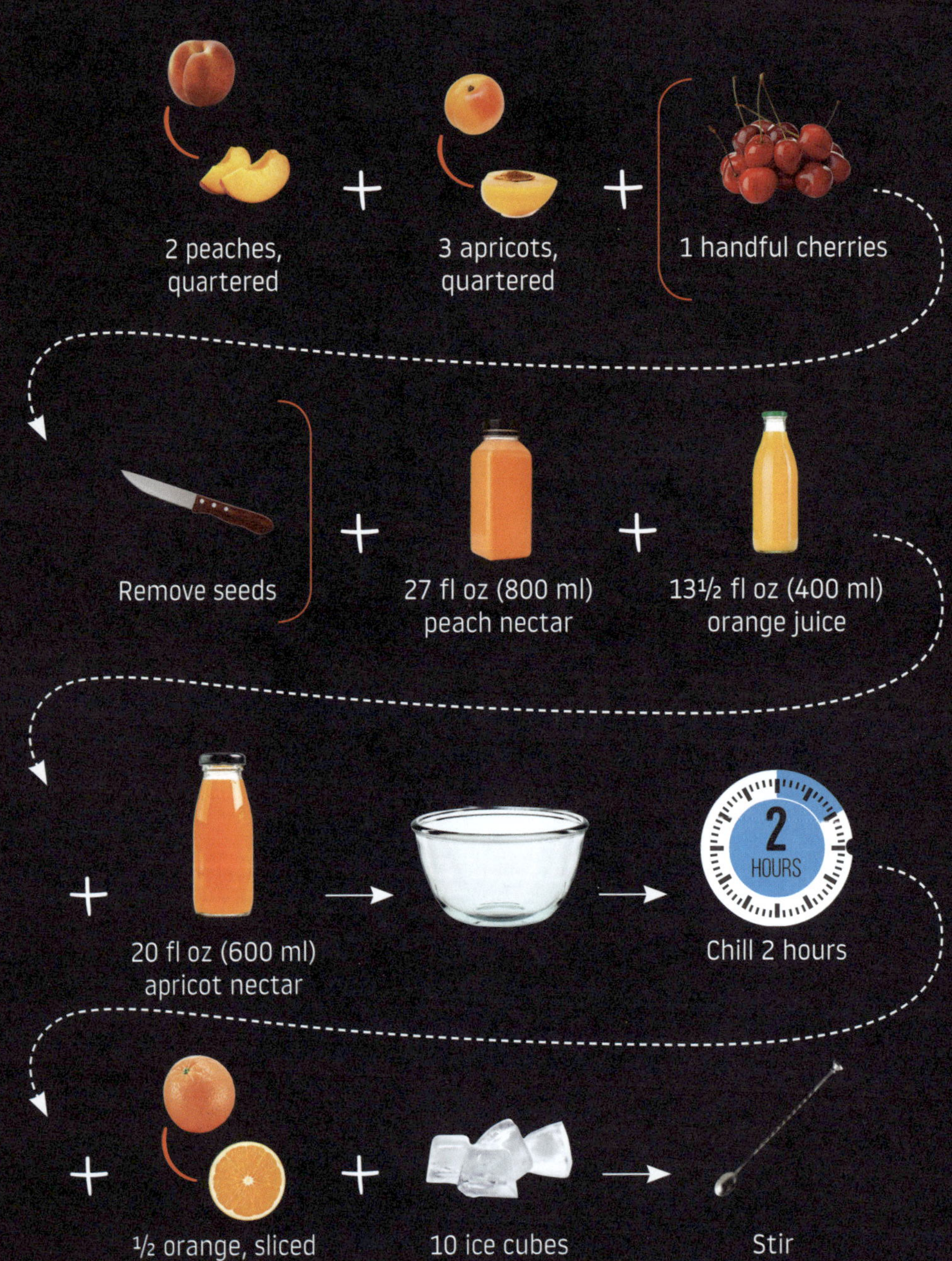

2 peaches, quartered
+
3 apricots, quartered
+
1 handful cherries
Remove seeds
+
27 fl oz (800 ml) peach nectar
+
13½ fl oz (400 ml) orange juice
+
20 fl oz (600 ml) apricot nectar
2 HOURS
Chill 2 hours
+
½ orange, sliced
+
10 ice cubes
Stir

MAKES 61 FL OZ (1.8 LITRES)
PREPARATION: 10 MINUTES
CHILLING: 2 HOURS

- 2 peaches, quartered
- 3 apricots, quartered
- 1 handful cherries, seeded
- 27 fl oz (800 ml) peach nectar
- 13½ fl oz (400 ml) orange juice
- 20 fl oz (600 ml) apricot nectar
- ½ orange, cut into slices
- 10 ice cubes

55 REFRESH

cucumber, apple and chilli

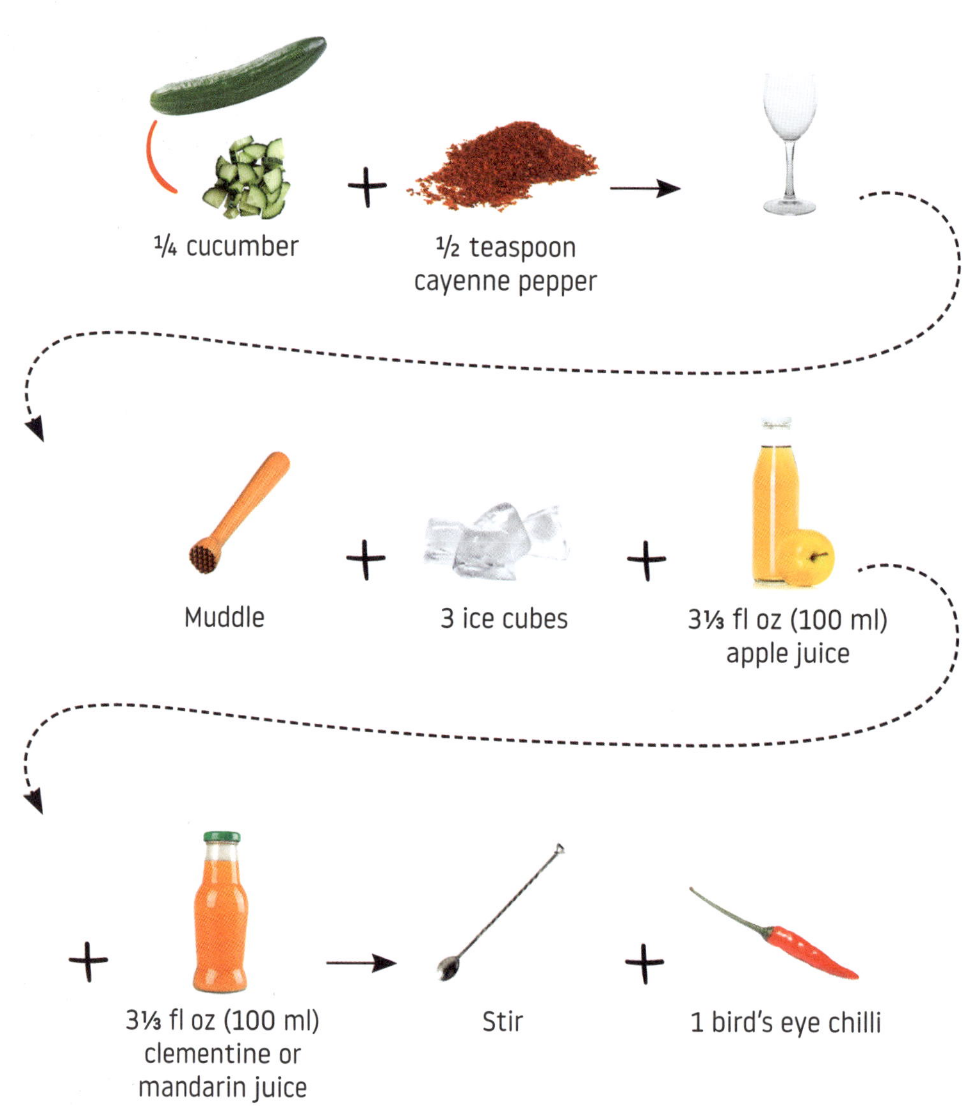

¼ cucumber
½ teaspoon cayenne pepper
Muddle
3 ice cubes
3⅓ fl oz (100 ml) apple juice
3⅓ fl oz (100 ml) clementine or mandarin juice
Stir
1 bird's eye chilli

MAKES 1 GLASS
PREPARATION: 5 MINUTES

- ¼ cucumber, diced
- ½ teaspoon cayenne pepper
- 3 ice cubes
- 3⅓ fl oz (100 ml) apple juice
- 3⅓ fl oz (100 ml) clementine or mandarin juice

56 VIRGIN LIGHT COLADA

coconut and pineapple

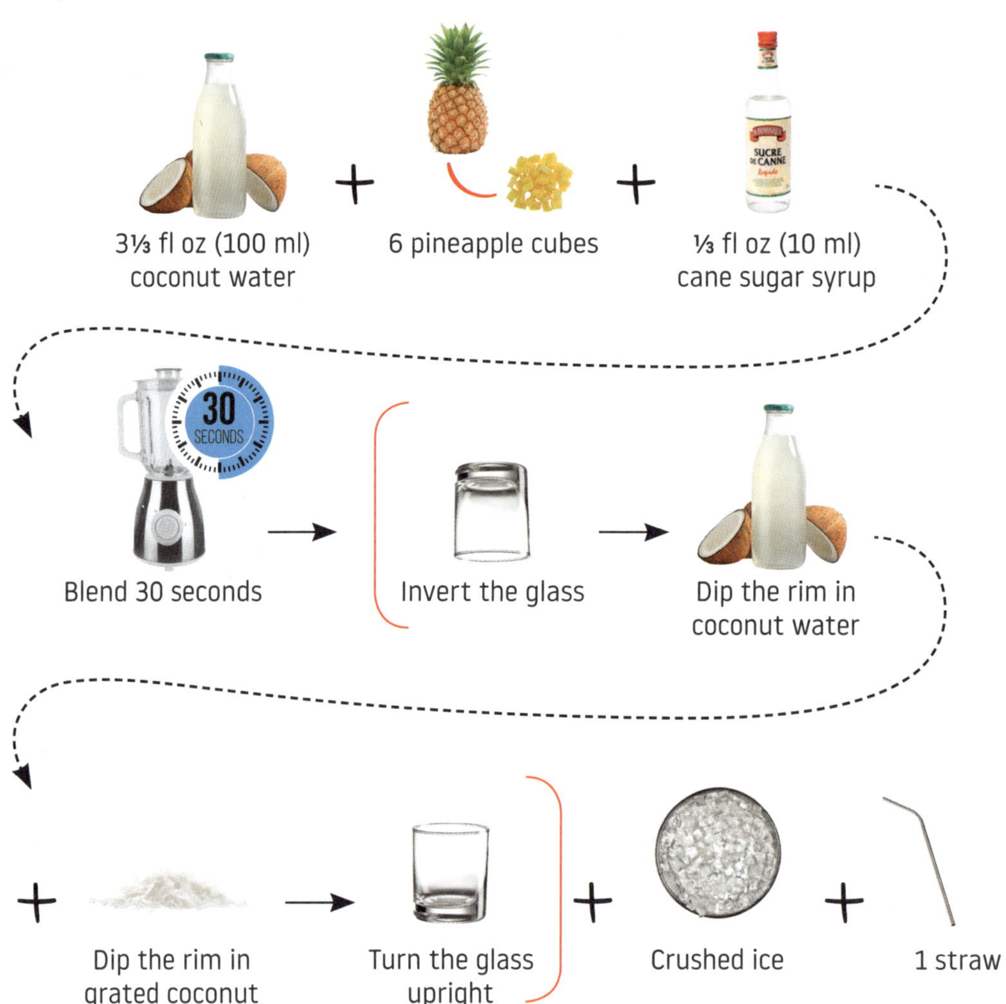

SUCRE DE CANNE
30 SECONDS
3⅓ fl oz (100 ml) coconut water
6 pineapple cubes
⅓ fl oz (10 ml) cane sugar syrup
Blend 30 seconds
Invert the glass
Dip the rim in coconut water
Dip the rim in grated coconut
Turn the glass upright
Crushed ice
1 straw

MAKES 1 GLASS
PREPARATION: 5 MINUTES

- 3⅓ fl oz (100 ml) coconut water + 1 tablespoon
- 6 pineapple cubes
- ⅓ fl oz (10 ml) cane sugar syrup
- grated coconut
- crushed ice

57 FLORENTINE

apple, cucumber and tarragon

¼ cucumber
+
1⅔ fl oz
(50 ml) water
Blend
Strain
Remove
1 fl oz (30 ml)
+
½ egg white
+
1 tarragon stem
+
1 teaspoon white
balsamic vinegar
+
1⅔ fl oz (50 ml)
apple juice
+
4 ice cubes
Shake vigorously
Strain
+
3 ice cubes
+
Lemonade
+
1 cucumber strip
+
A few tarragon
leaves

MAKES 1 GLASS
PREPARATION: 5 MINUTES

- ¼ cucumber, diced + 1 strip
- 1⅔ fl oz (50 ml) water
- ½ egg white (or ⅔ fl oz/20 ml aquafaba for a vegan mocktail)
- 1 tarragon stem
- 1 teaspoon white balsamic vinegar
- 1⅔ fl oz (50 ml) apple juice
- 7 ice cubes
- lemonade

58 BETTY BOOP

strawberry, cucumber and pear

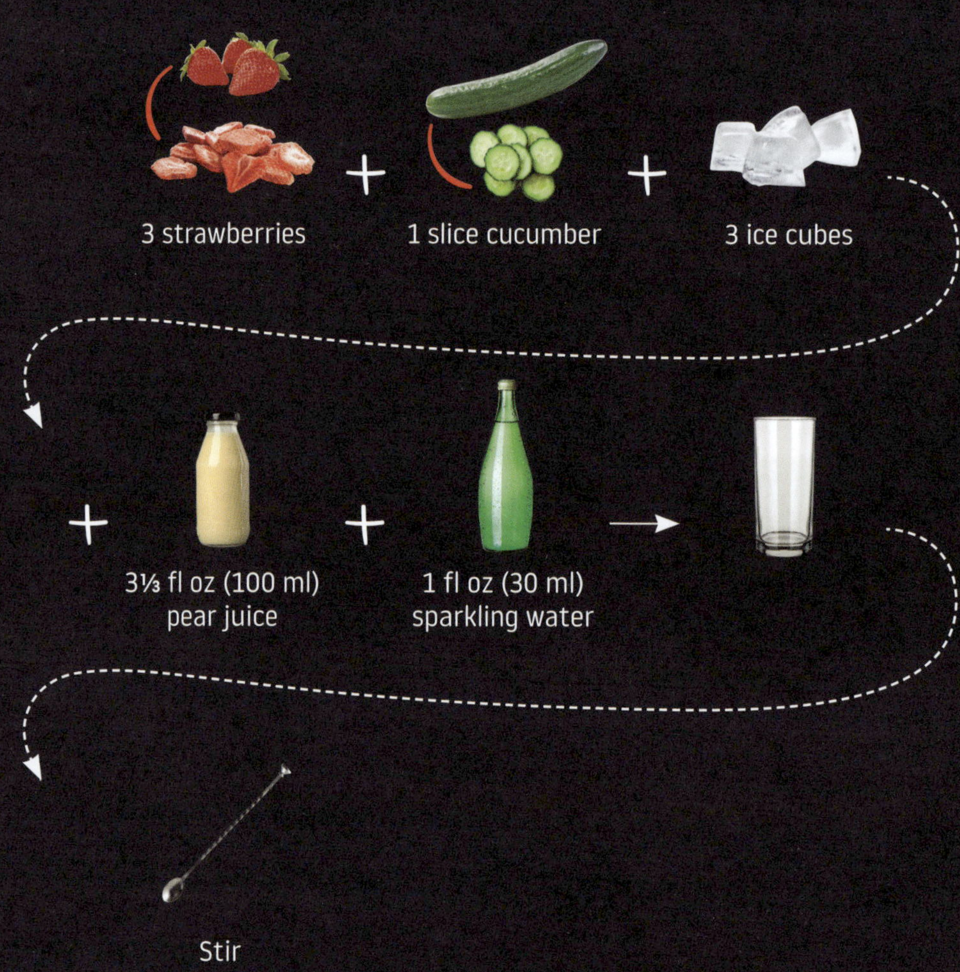

3 strawberries
1 slice cucumber
3 ice cubes
3⅓ fl oz (100 ml) pear juice
1 fl oz (30 ml) sparkling water
Stir

MAKES 1 GLASS
PREPARATION: 5 MINUTES

- 3 strawberries, sliced
- 1 slice cucumber
- 3 ice cubes
- 3⅓ fl oz (100 ml) pear juice
- 1 fl oz (30 ml) sparkling water

59 GREEN SMOOTHIE

avocado, apple and kiwifruit

½ avocado
1 Granny Smith apple
1 kiwifruit
20 SECONDS
5 fl oz (150 ml) milk
3 ice cubes
Blend 20 seconds
1 slice kiwifruit
1 straw

MAKES 1 GLASS
PREPARATION: 5 MINUTES

- ½ avocado, diced
- 1 Granny Smith apple, diced
- 1 kiwifruit, sliced + 1 slice
- 5 fl oz (150 ml) milk
- 3 ice cubes

60 WELCOME TO PARADISE

beetroot, passionfruit and raspberry

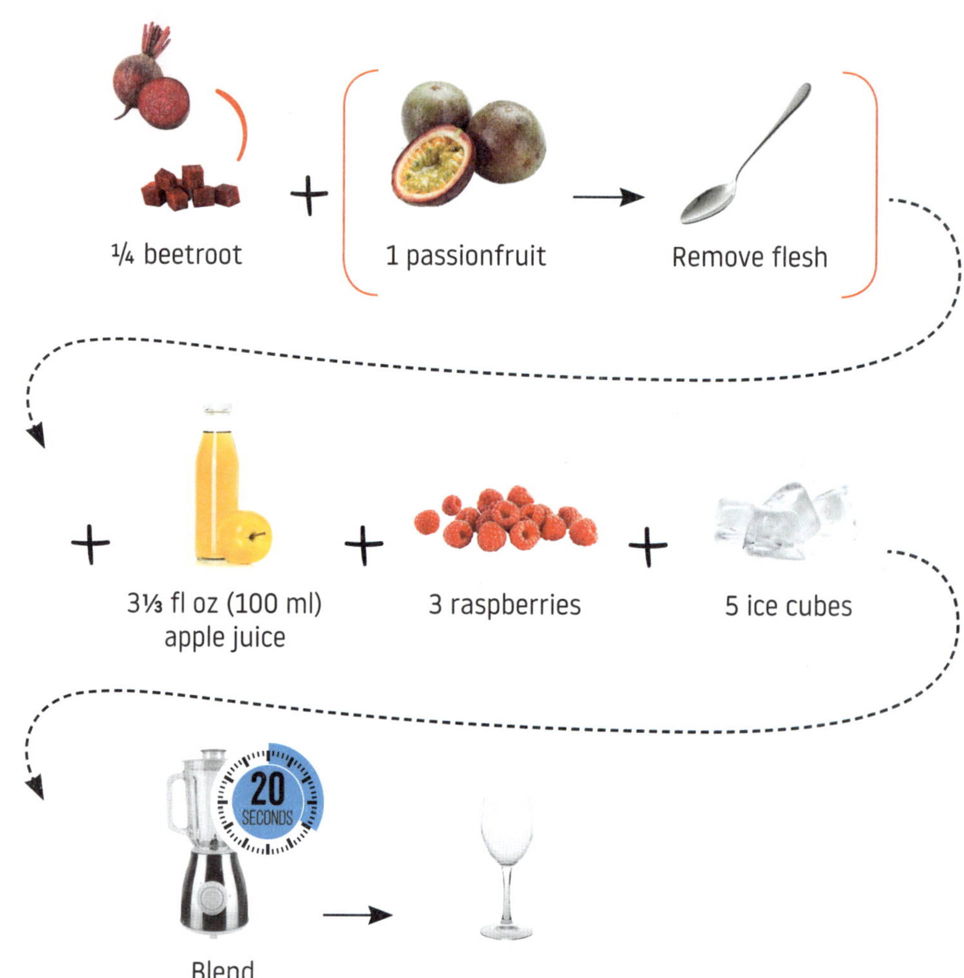

¼ beetroot
1 passionfruit
Remove flesh
3⅓ fl oz (100 ml) apple juice
3 raspberries
5 ice cubes
20 SECONDS
Blend

MAKES 1 GLASS
PREPARATION: 5 MINUTES

- ¼ beetroot, diced
- 1 passionfruit, flesh removed
- 3⅓ fl oz (100 ml) apple juice
- 3 raspberries
- 5 ice cubes

61 DO BRAZIL

pineapple, passionfruit and orange

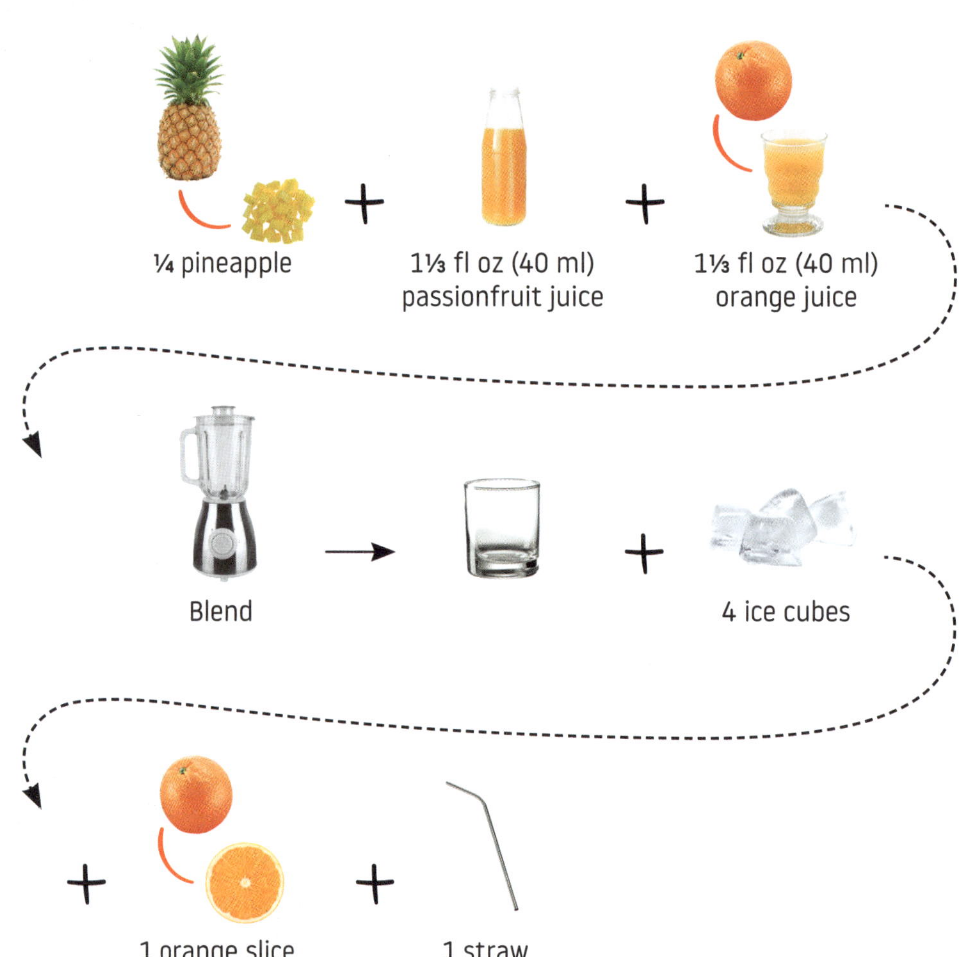

¼ pineapple
1⅓ fl oz (40 ml) passionfruit juice
1⅓ fl oz (40 ml) orange juice
Blend
4 ice cubes
1 orange slice
1 straw

MAKES 1 GLASS
PREPARATION: 5 MINUTES

- ¼ pineapple, diced
- 1⅓ fl oz (40 ml) passionfruit juice
- 1⅓ fl oz (40 ml) orange juice
- 4 ice cubes
- 1 orange slice

62 INFERNO KISS

capsicum, strawberry and spices

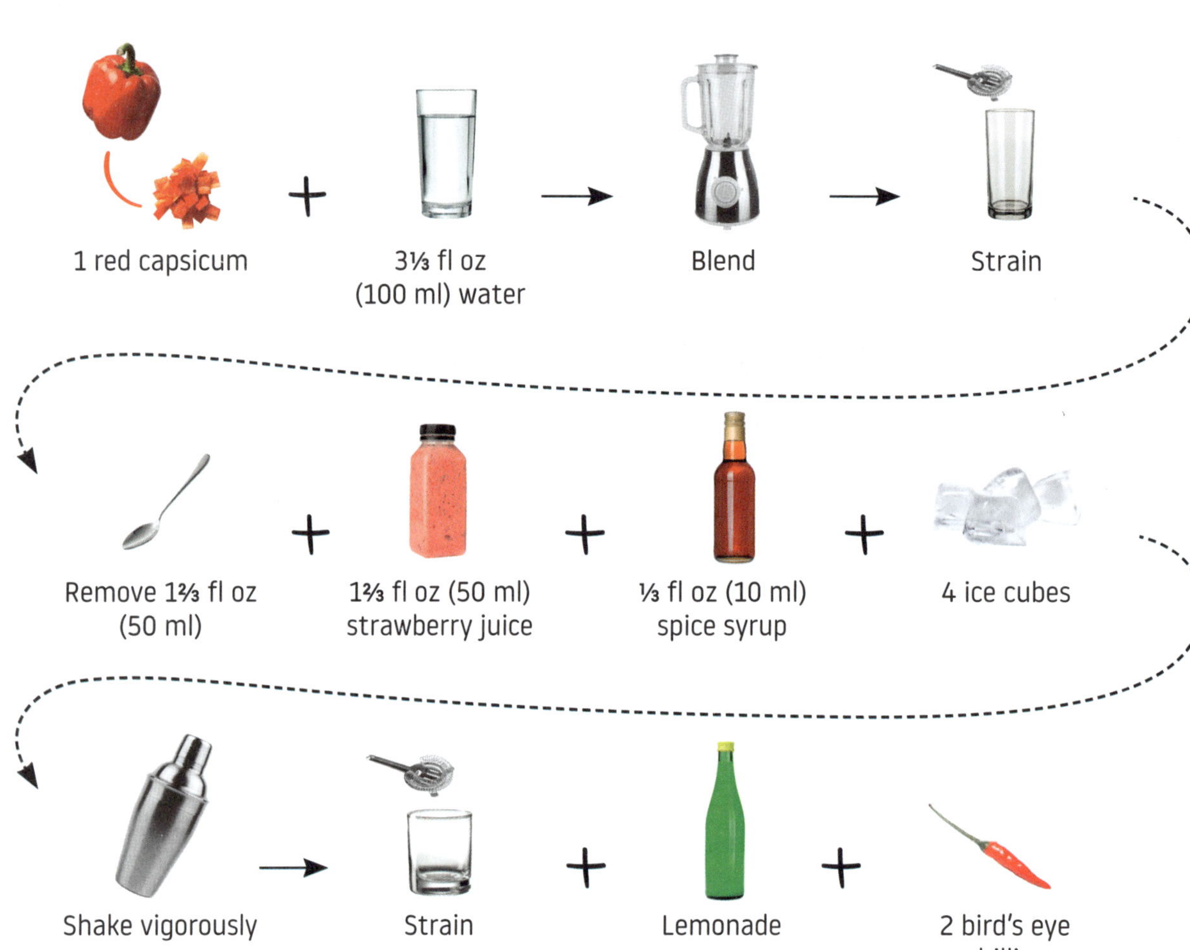

1 red capsicum
3⅓ fl oz
(100 ml) water
Blend
Strain
Remove 1⅔ fl oz
(50 ml)
1⅔ fl oz (50 ml)
strawberry juice
⅓ fl oz (10 ml)
spice syrup
4 ice cubes
Shake vigorously
Strain
Lemonade
2 bird's eye
chillies

MAKES 1 GLASS
PREPARATION: 5 MINUTES

- 1 red capsicum, seeded and diced
- 3⅓ fl oz (100 ml) water
- 1⅔ fl oz (50 ml) strawberry juice
- ⅓ fl oz (10 ml) spice syrup
- 4 ice cubes
- lemonade
- 2 bird's eye chillies

63 CINNAMON SERENITY

clementine, pear and cinnamon

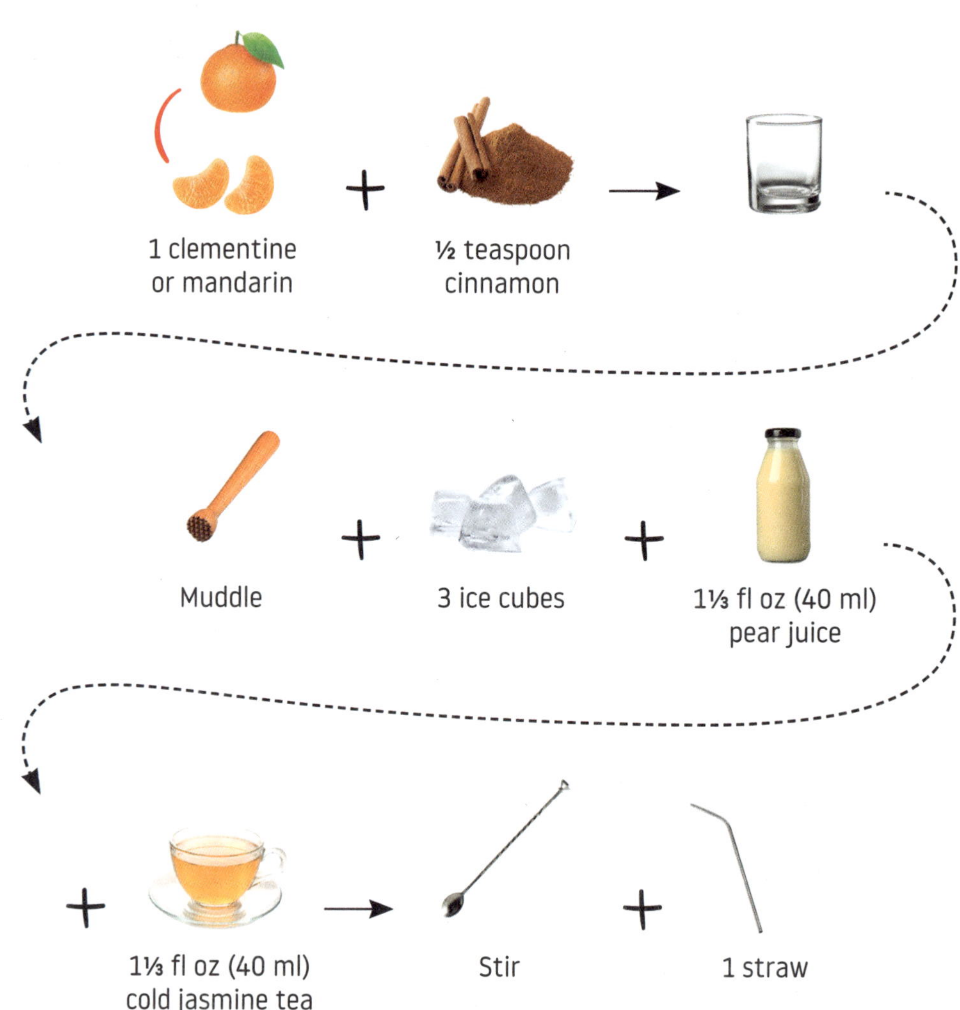
1 clementine
or mandarin
+
½ teaspoon
cinnamon
Muddle
+
3 ice cubes
+
1⅓ fl oz (40 ml)
pear juice
+
1⅓ fl oz (40 ml)
cold jasmine tea
Stir
+
1 straw

MAKES 1 GLASS
PREPARATION: 5 MINUTES

- 1 clementine or mandarin, peeled and segmented
- ½ teaspoon cinnamon
- 3 ice cubes
- 1⅓ fl oz (40 ml) pear juice
- 1⅓ fl oz (40 ml) cold jasmine tea

64 FABULOUS RIO

passionfruit and caramelised pineapple

½ passionfruit
Remove flesh
½ fl oz (15 ml) caramelised pineapple syrup
⅓ fl oz (10 ml) lime juice
⅔ fl oz (20 ml) pineapple juice
1⅓ fl oz (40 ml) acai and guarana tea blend
4 ice cubes
Shake vigorously
1 piece caramelised pineapple
Cut
Pinch lime zest

MAKES 1 GLASS
PREPARATION: 5 MINUTES

- ½ passionfruit, flesh removed
- ½ fl oz (15 ml) caramelised pineapple syrup
- ⅓ fl oz (10 ml) lime juice
- ⅔ fl oz (20 ml) pineapple juice
- 1⅓ fl oz (40 ml) acai and guarana tea blend
- 4 ice cubes
- 1 piece caramelised pineapple
- pinch lime zest

65 PEACH SUNSET

apricot, peach and orange

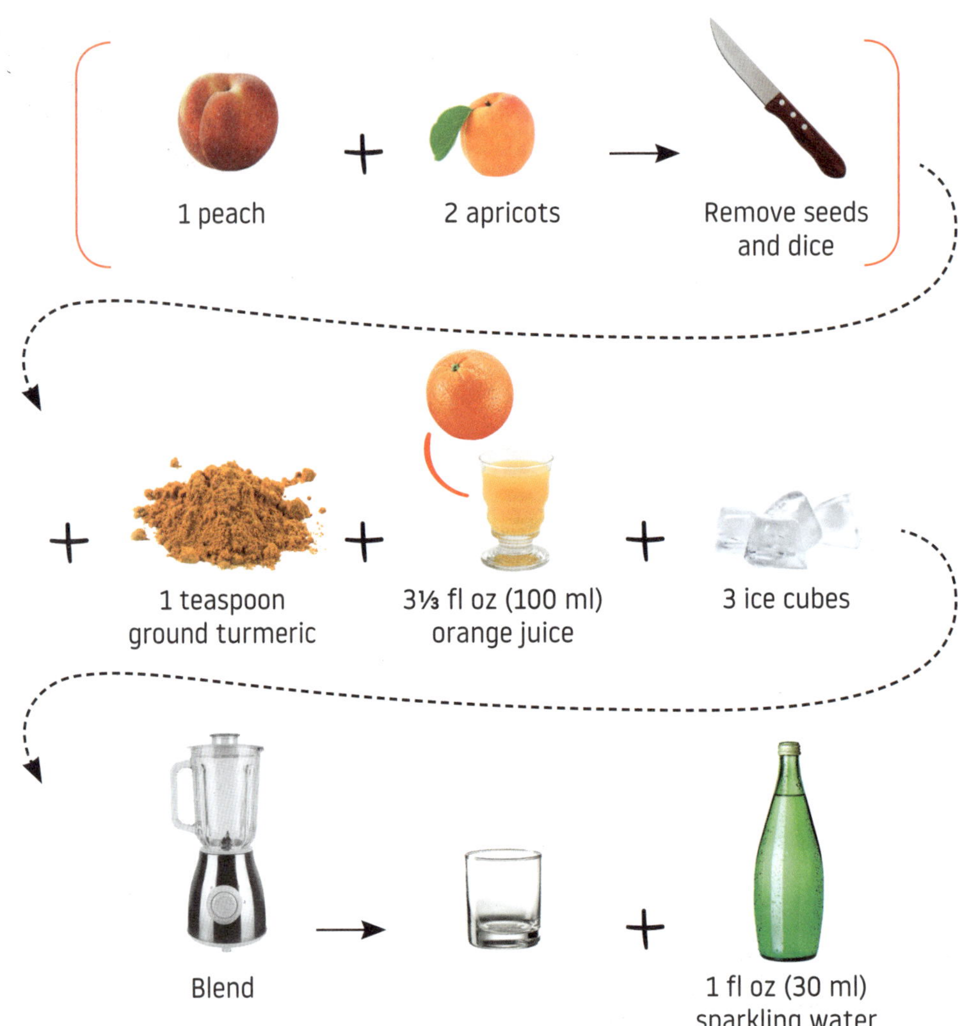
1 peach
2 apricots
Remove seeds and dice
1 teaspoon ground turmeric
3⅓ fl oz (100 ml) orange juice
3 ice cubes
Blend
1 fl oz (30 ml) sparkling water

MAKES 1 GLASS
PREPARATION: 5 MINUTES

- 1 peach, seeded and diced
- 2 apricots, seeded and diced
- 1 teaspoon ground turmeric
- 3⅓ fl oz (100 ml) orange juice
- 3 ice cubes
- 1 fl oz (30 ml) sparkling water

66 KIWI CUCUMBER
cooler

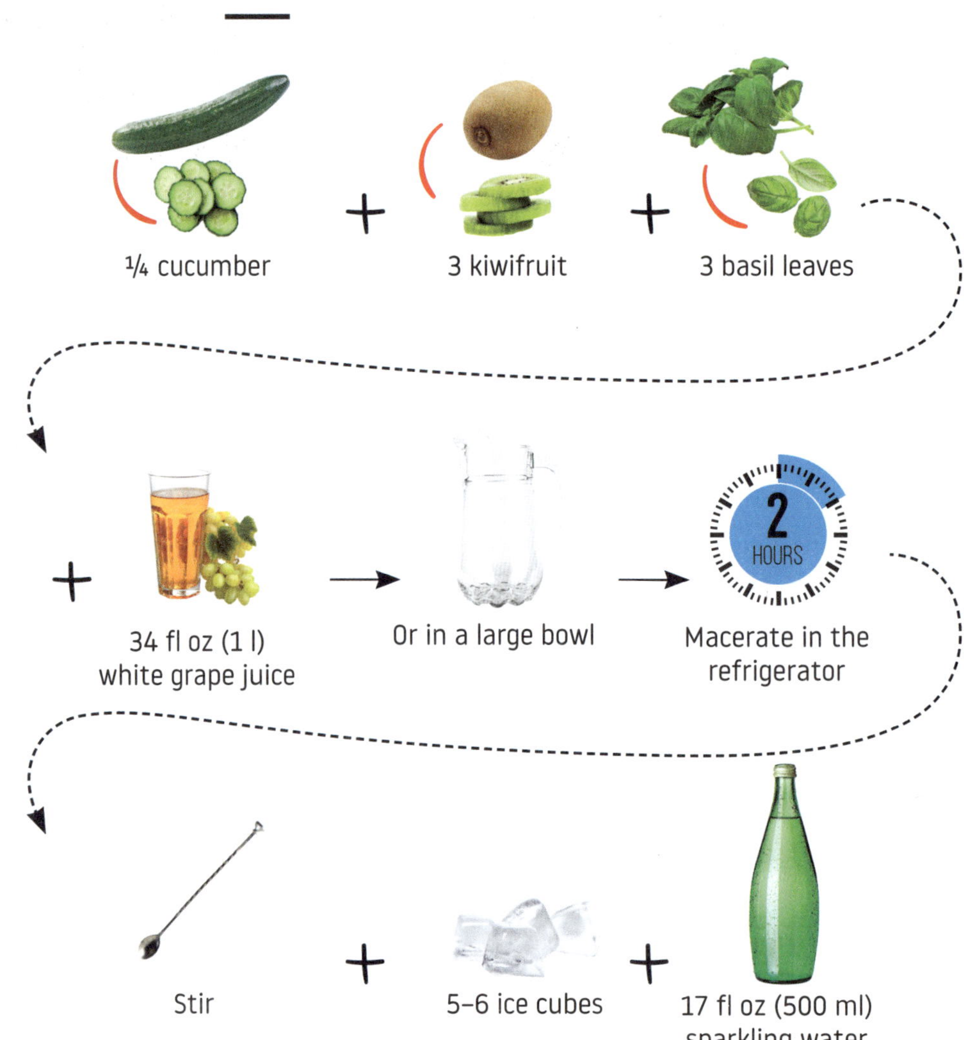

¼ cucumber
3 kiwifruit
3 basil leaves
34 fl oz (1 l)
white grape juice
Or in a large bowl
2
HOURS
Macerate in the
refrigerator
Stir
5–6 ice cubes
17 fl oz (500 ml)
sparkling water

51 FL OZ (1.5 LITRES)
PREPARATION: 10 MINUTES
MACERATION: 2 HOURS

- ¼ cucumber, sliced
- 3 kiwifruit, sliced
- 3 basil leaves
- 34 fl oz (1 l) white grape juice
- 5–6 ice cubes
- 17 fl oz (500 ml) sparkling water

67 MAJORELLE'S GARDEN

green tea and floral water

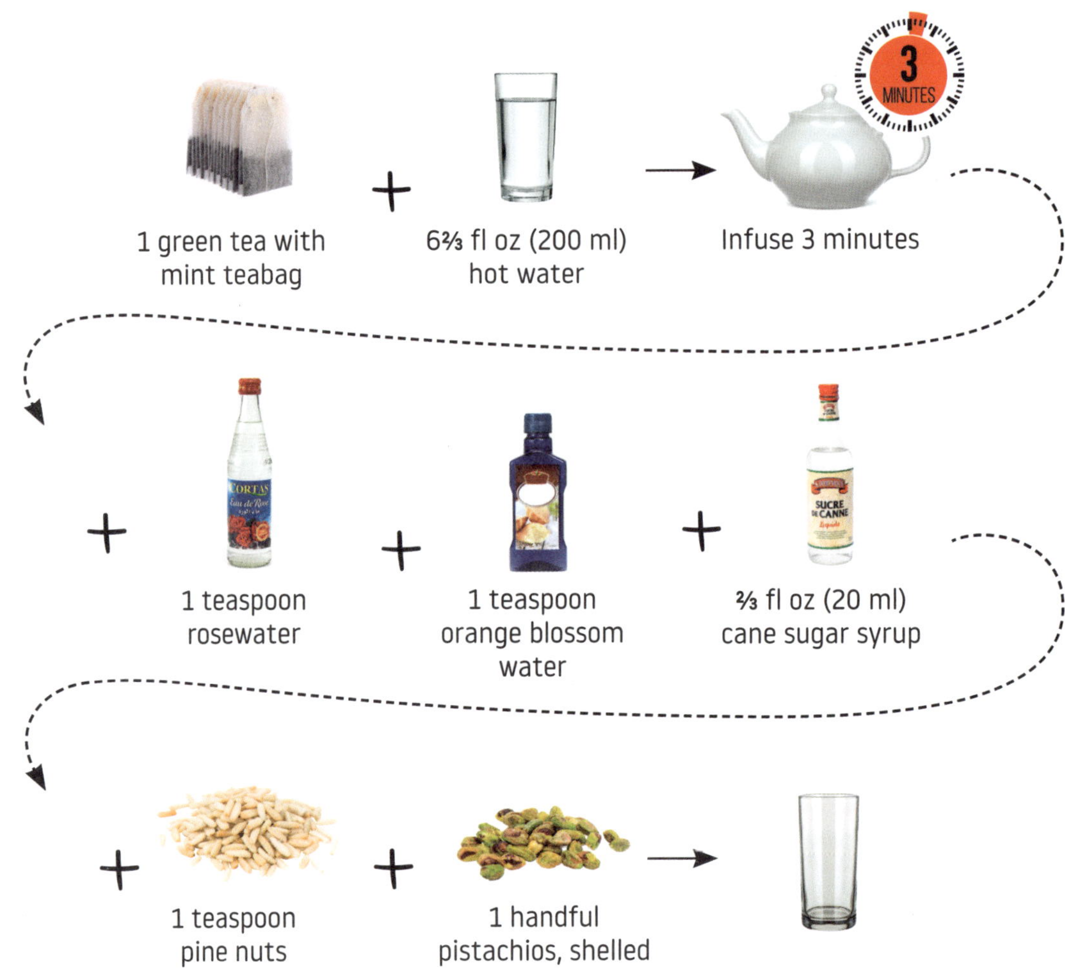
3
MINUTES
1 green tea with mint teabag
6⅔ fl oz (200 ml) hot water
Infuse 3 minutes
1 teaspoon rosewater
1 teaspoon orange blossom water
⅔ fl oz (20 ml) cane sugar syrup
1 teaspoon pine nuts
1 handful pistachios, shelled

MAKES 1 GLASS
PREPARATION: 3 MINUTES
INFUSING: 3 MINUTES

- 1 green tea with mint teabag
- 6⅔ fl oz (200 ml) hot water
- 1 teaspoon rosewater
- 1 teaspoon orange blossom water
- ⅔ fl oz (20 ml) cane sugar syrup
- 1 teaspoon pine nuts
- 1 handful pistachios, shelled and diced

68 ACAI DELIGHT

strawberry and basil

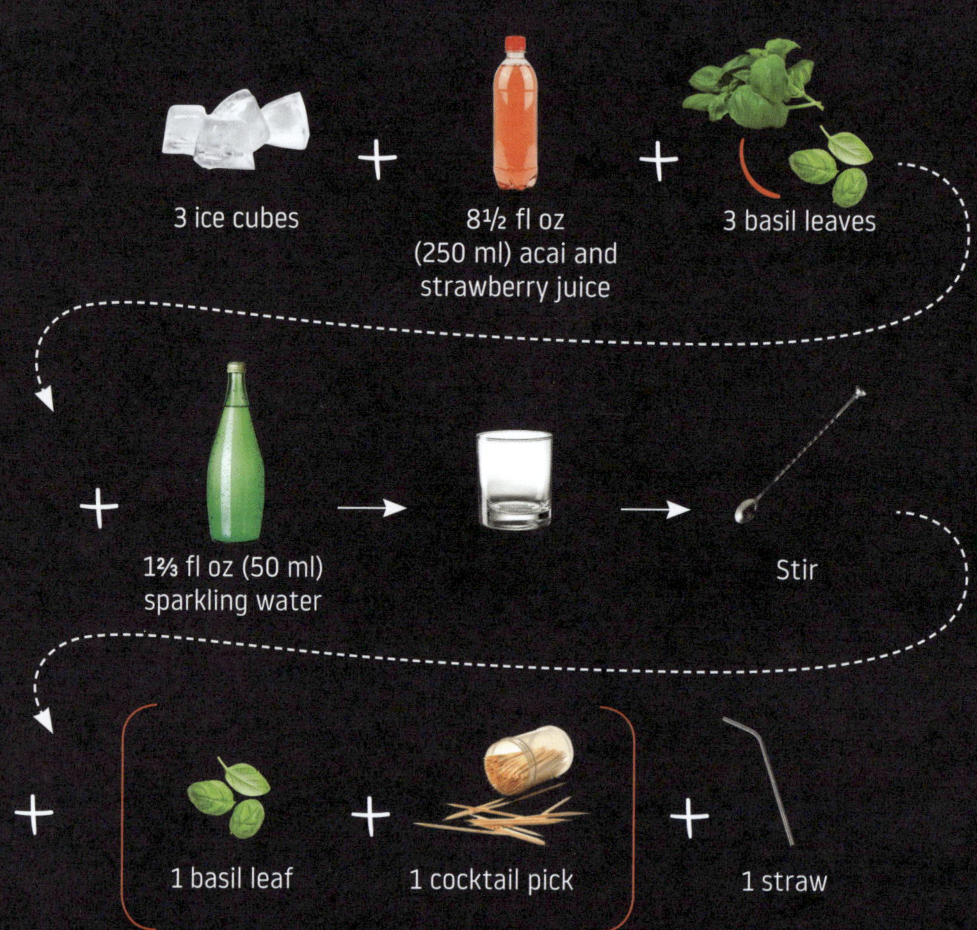
3 ice cubes
+
8½ fl oz (250 ml) acai and strawberry juice
+
3 basil leaves
+
1⅔ fl oz (50 ml) sparkling water
Stir
+
1 basil leaf
+
1 cocktail pick
+
1 straw

MAKES 1 GLASS
PREPARATION: 5 MINUTES

- 3 ice cubes
- 8½ fl oz (250 ml) strawberry and acai juice
- 4 basil leaves
- 1⅔ fl oz (50 ml) sparkling water

69 DAISY DELIGHT

cucumber and lychee

¼ cucumber
+
1⅔ fl oz
(50 ml) water
Blend
Strain
Remove 1 fl oz
(30 ml)
+
1 fl oz (30 ml)
lychee juice
+
1 ice cube
Stir
+
Lemonade
Stir
+
A few
cucumber slices

MAKES 1 GLASS
PREPARATION: 5 MINUTES

- ¼ cucumber, diced
  + a few slices
- 1⅔ fl oz (50 ml) water
- 1 fl oz (30 ml) lychee juice
- 1 ice cube
- lemonade

70 SAN ITALIA

orange and grapefruit

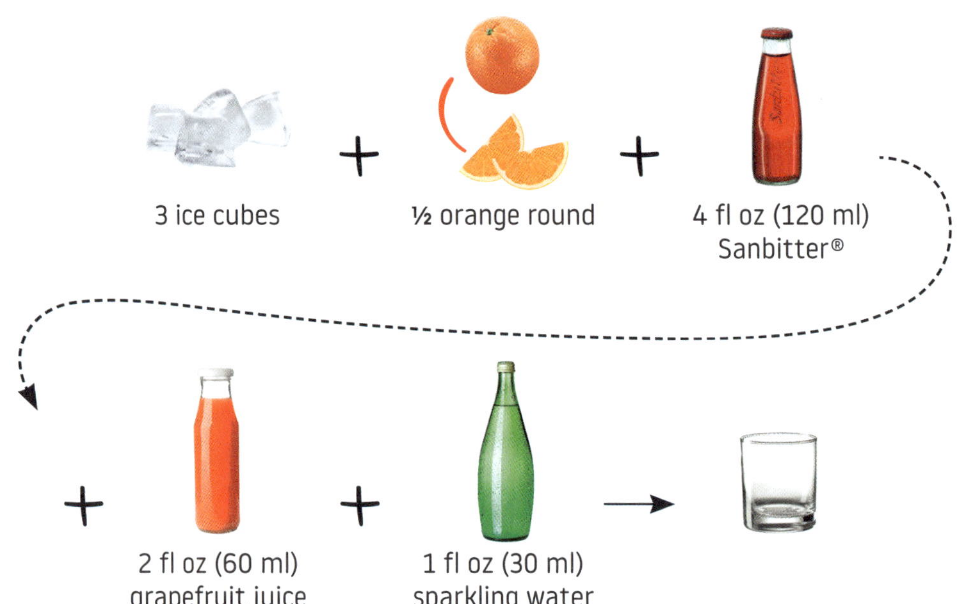
3 ice cubes
½ orange round
4 fl oz (120 ml) Sanbitter®
2 fl oz (60 ml) grapefruit juice
1 fl oz (30 ml) sparkling water

SANBITTER

MAKES 1 GLASS
PREPARATION: 5 MINUTES

- 3 ice cubes
- ½ orange round
- 4 fl oz (120 ml) Sanbitter®
  or sparkling orange soda
- 2 fl oz (60 ml) grapefruit juice
- 1 fl oz (30 ml) sparkling water

71 FRESH GREEN TEA

grapes, lime and birch

1 lime
6 sprigs mint
1 bunch white grapes
10 ice cubes
2 limes, juiced
6⅔ fl oz (200 ml) white grape juice
3⅓ fl oz (100 ml) birch sap or maple syrup
Stir
34 fl oz (1 l) cold green tea
Stir

SERVES 10
PREPARATION: 5 MINUTES

- 1 lime, sliced + 2 limes, juiced
- 6 sprigs mint
- 1 bunch of white grapes
- 10 ice cubes
- 6⅔ fl oz (200 ml) white grape juice
- 3⅓ fl oz (100 ml) birch sap or maple syrup
- 34 fl oz (1 l) cold green tea

72 MOCKTAIL RIO

fruit and spices

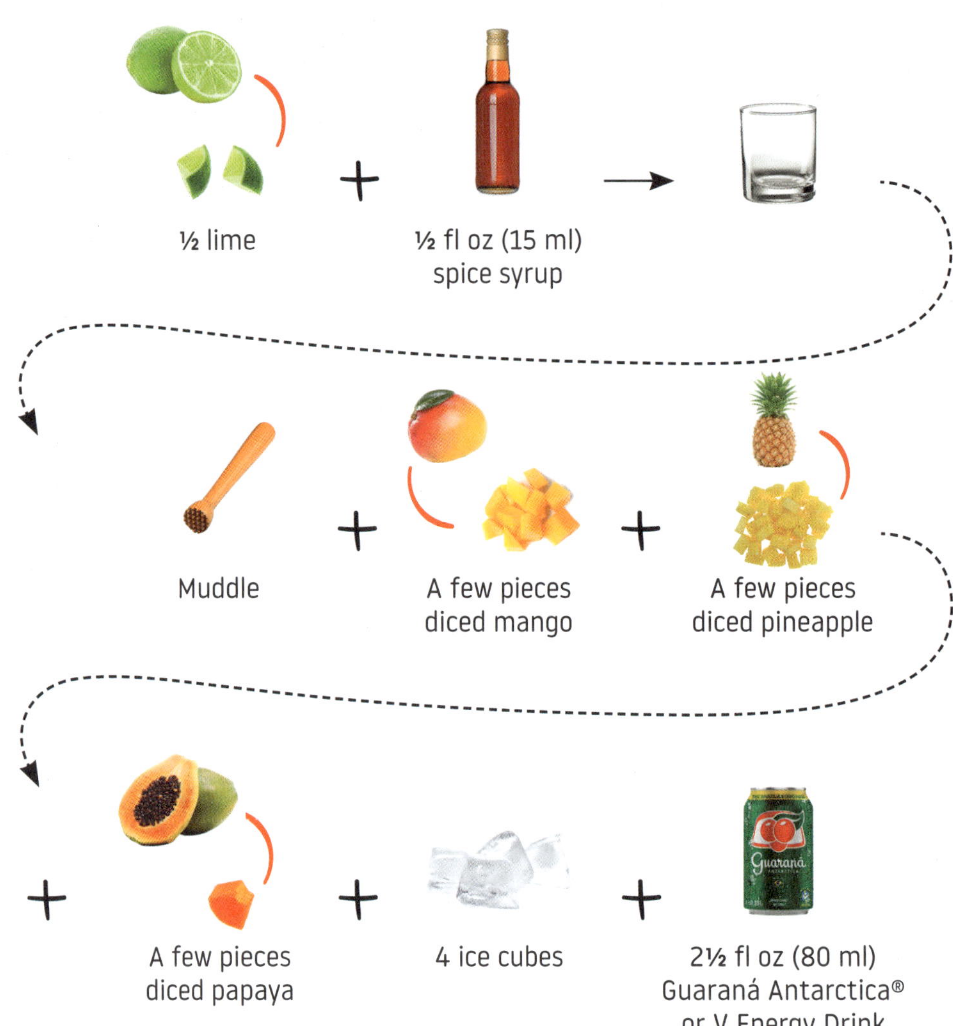

½ lime
½ fl oz (15 ml)
spice syrup
Muddle
A few pieces
diced mango
A few pieces
diced pineapple
A few pieces
diced papaya
4 ice cubes
2½ fl oz (80 ml)
Guaraná Antarctica®
or V Energy Drink
Guaraná

Guaraná
ANTARCTICA

MAKES 1 GLASS
PREPARATION: 5 MINUTES

- ½ lime, diced
- ½ fl oz (15 ml) spice syrup
- a few pieces diced mango
- a few pieces diced pineapple
- a few pieces diced papaya
- 4 ice cubes
- 2½ fl oz (80 ml) Guaraná Antarctica® or V Energy Drink

73 PUSSYFOOT JOHNSON

citrus and grenadine

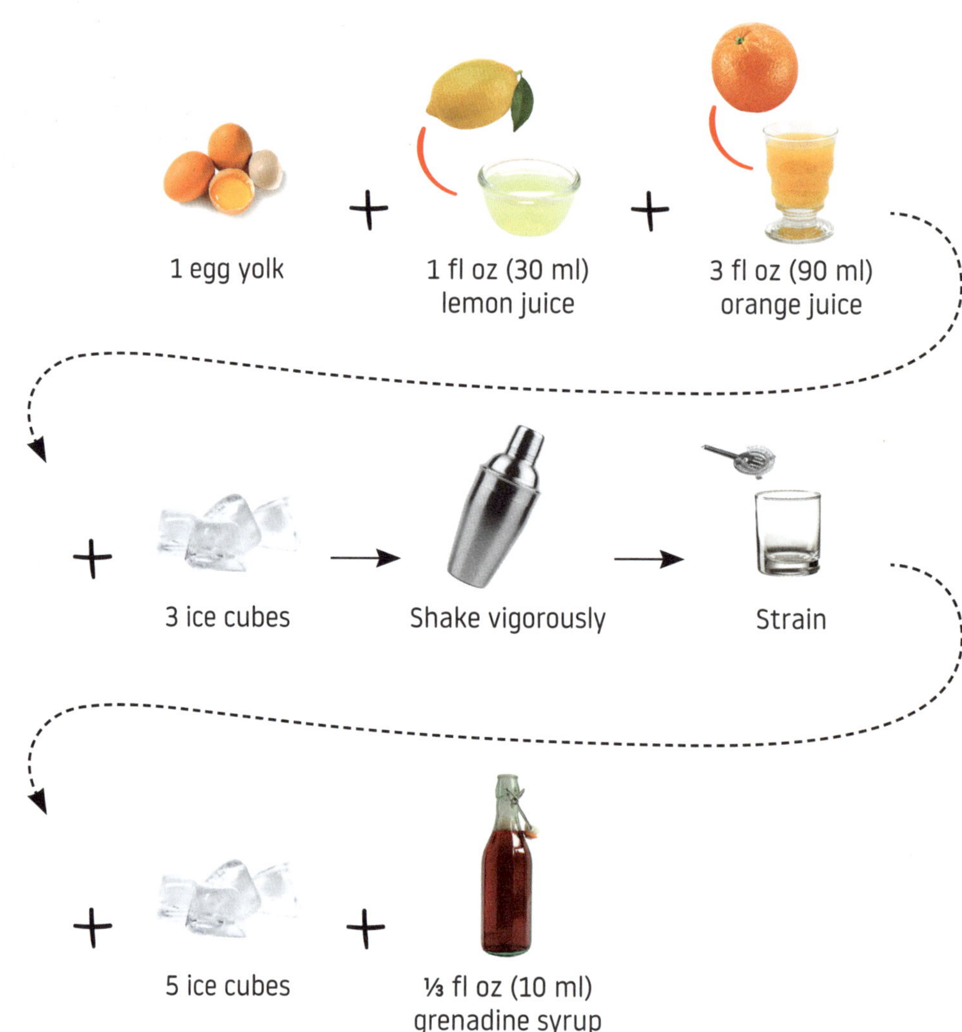
1 egg yolk
1 fl oz (30 ml) lemon juice
3 fl oz (90 ml) orange juice
3 ice cubes
Shake vigorously
Strain
5 ice cubes
⅓ fl oz (10 ml) grenadine syrup

MAKES 1 GLASS
PREPARATION: 5 MINUTES

- 1 egg yolk
- 1 fl oz (30 ml) lemon juice
- 3 fl oz (90 ml) orange juice
- 8 ice cubes
- ⅓ fl oz (10 ml) grenadine syrup

74 BILLABONG

strawberry, lychee and melon

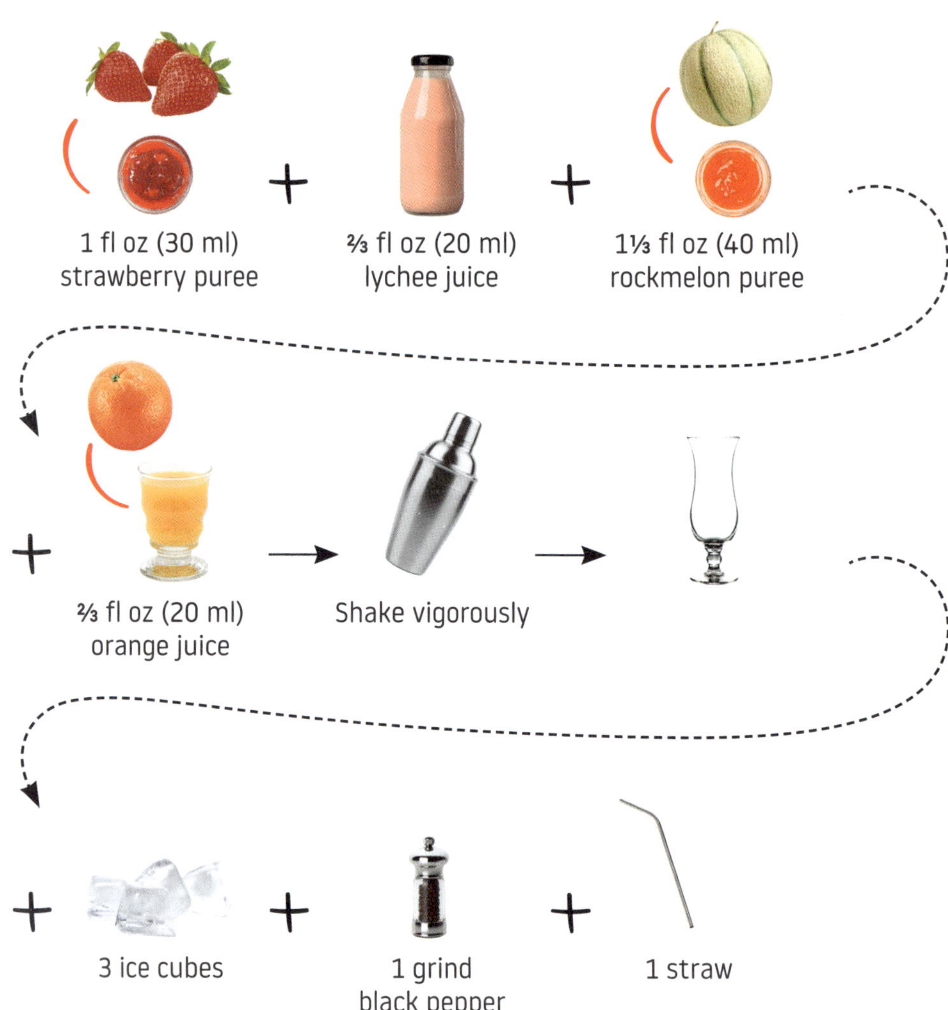

1 fl oz (30 ml)
strawberry puree
⅔ fl oz (20 ml)
lychee juice
1⅓ fl oz (40 ml)
rockmelon puree
⅔ fl oz (20 ml)
orange juice
Shake vigorously
3 ice cubes
1 grind
black pepper
1 straw

MAKES 1 GLASS
PREPARATION: 5 MINUTES

- 1 fl oz (30 ml) strawberry puree
- ⅔ fl oz (20 ml) lychee juice
- 1⅓ fl oz (40 ml) rockmelon puree
- ⅔ fl oz (20 ml) orange juice
- 3 ice cubes
- 1 grind black pepper

75 SPICED
Milky Way

10 cacao beans
+
10 fl oz (300 ml) coconut water
→
Blend
+
34 fl oz (1 l) chocolate soy milk
+
1 pinch nutmeg
+
1 pinch cinnamon
+
34 fl oz (1 l) hazelnut milk
→
Blend again
→
+
15 ice cubes
+
5 star anise

78 FL OZ (2.3 LITRES)
PREPARATION: 10 MINUTES

- 10 cacao beans
- 10 fl oz (300 ml) coconut water
- 34 fl oz (1 l) chocolate soy milk
- 1 pinch nutmeg
- 1 pinch cinnamon
- 34 fl oz (1 l) hazelnut milk
- 15 ice cubes
- 5 star anise

76 RISING SUN

rice milk, mango and goji berries

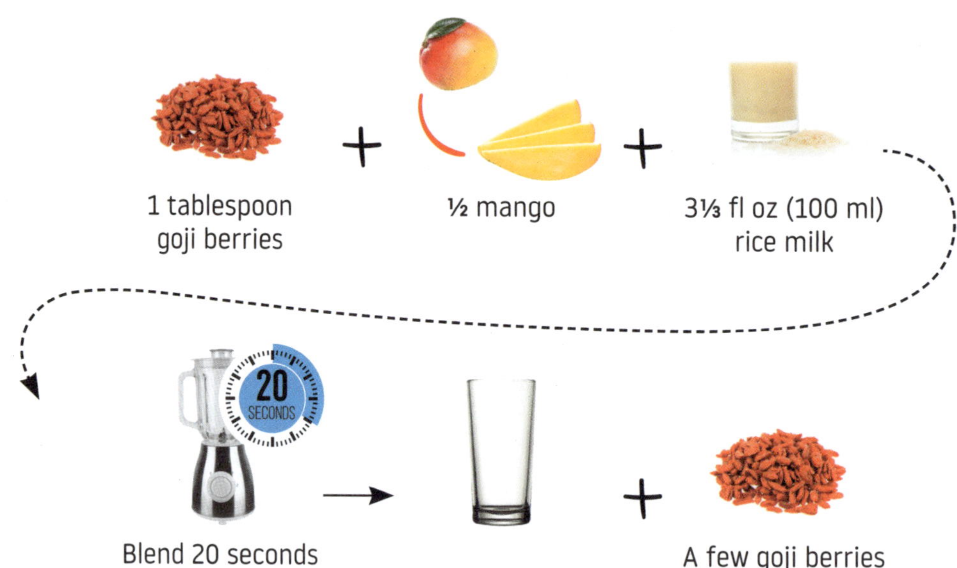
1 tablespoon goji berries
½ mango
3⅓ fl oz (100 ml) rice milk
20 SECONDS
Blend 20 seconds
A few goji berries

MAKES 1 GLASS
PREPARATION: 5 MINUTES

- 1 tablespoon goji berries + a few berries
- ½ mango, sliced
- 3⅓ fl oz (100 ml) rice milk

77 INVIGORATING MOCKTAIL

avocado, apple and lime

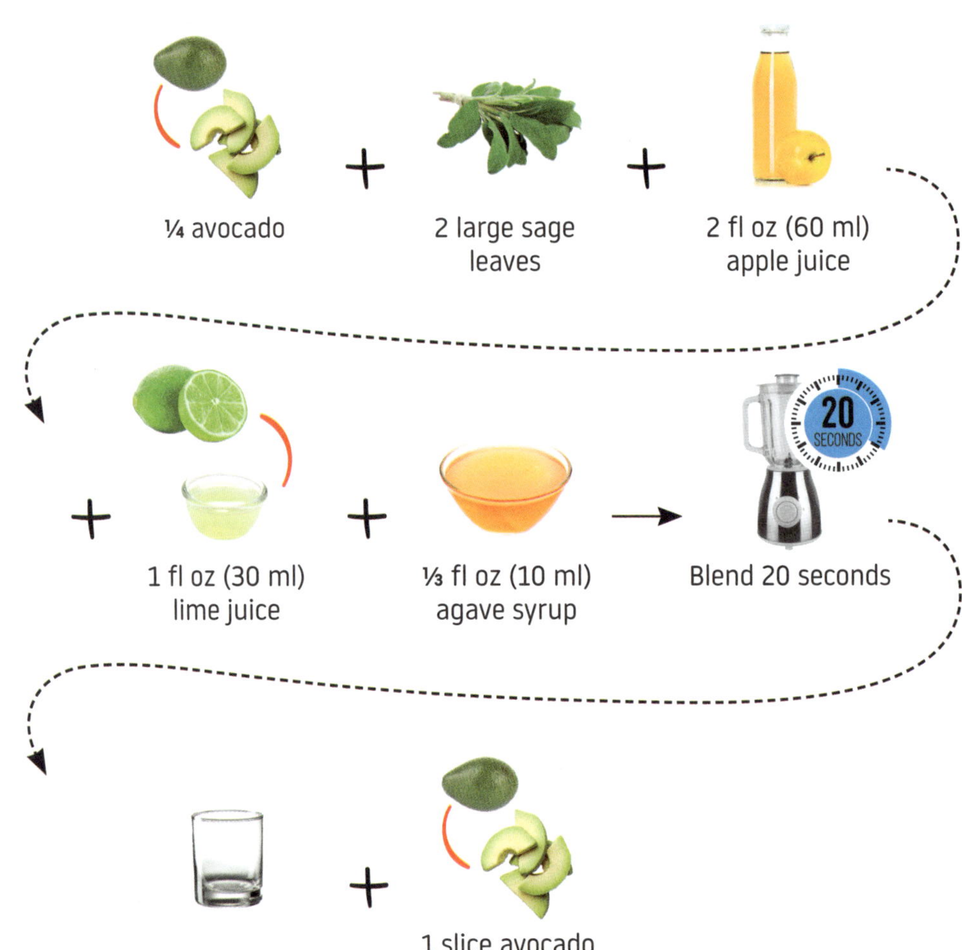
¼ avocado
2 large sage leaves
2 fl oz (60 ml) apple juice
1 fl oz (30 ml) lime juice
⅓ fl oz (10 ml) agave syrup
20 SECONDS
Blend 20 seconds
1 slice avocado

MAKES 1 GLASS
PREPARATION: 5 MINUTES

- ¼ avocado, sliced + 1 slice
- 2 large sage leaves
- 2 fl oz (60 ml) apple juice
- 1 fl oz (30 ml) lime juice
- ⅓ fl oz (10 ml) agave syrup

78 ENCHANTED GARDEN

tomato, capsicum and tea

7 oz (200 g)
cherry tomatoes
2 limes, juiced
1 yellow capsicum
Extract the juice
7 oz (200 g) sugar
34 fl oz (1 l) cold
Earl Grey tea
34 fl oz (1 l)
sparkling water
Crushed ice
Stir

MAKES 68 FL OZ (2 LITRES)
PREPARATION: 10 MINUTES

- 7 oz (200 g) cherry tomatoes, juiced
- 2 limes, juiced
- 1 yellow capsicum, juiced
- 7 oz (200 g) sugar
- 34 fl oz (1 l) cold Earl Grey tea
- 34 fl oz (1 l) sparkling water
- crushed ice

79 CHERRY ICED TEA

with mint and ginger

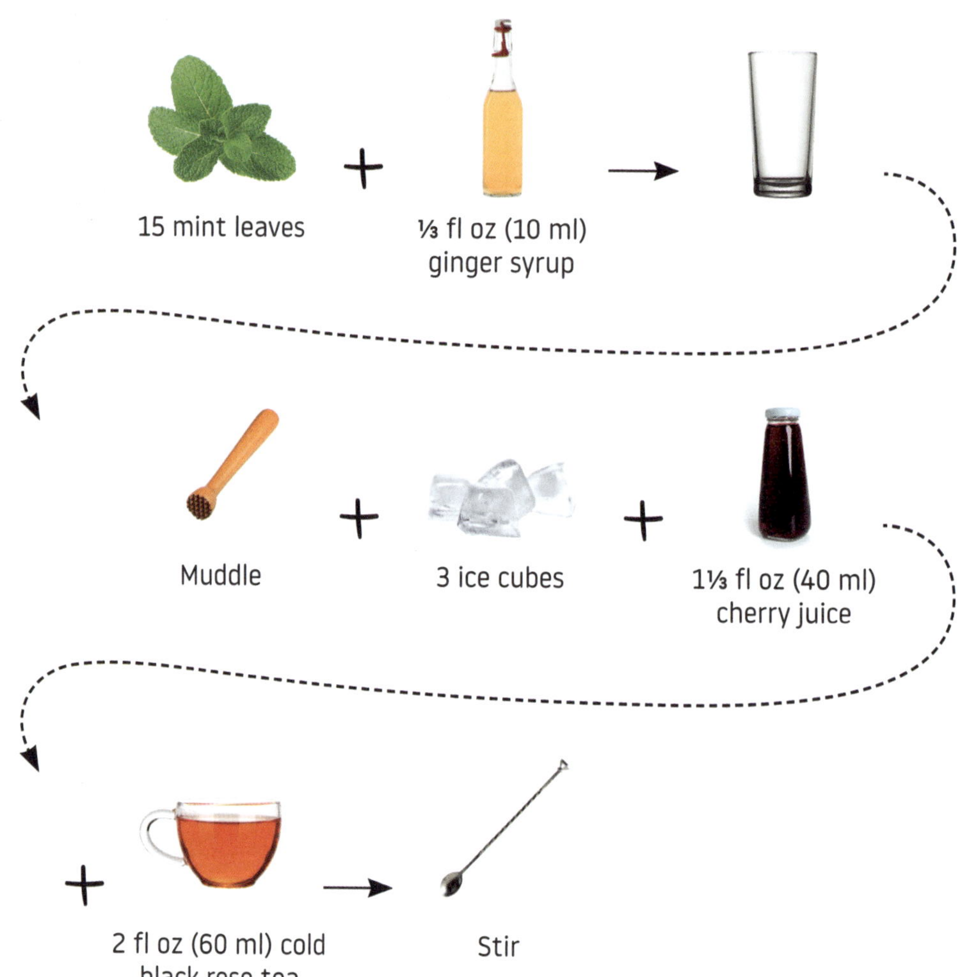
15 mint leaves
⅓ fl oz (10 ml) ginger syrup
Muddle
3 ice cubes
1⅓ fl oz (40 ml) cherry juice
2 fl oz (60 ml) cold black rose tea
Stir

MAKES 1 GLASS
PREPARATION: 5 MINUTES

- 15 mint leaves
- ⅓ fl oz (10 ml) ginger syrup
- 3 ice cubes
- 1⅓ fl oz (40 ml) cherry juice
- 2 fl oz (60 ml) cold black rose tea

80 AUTUMN SPIRIT

apple, pear and date

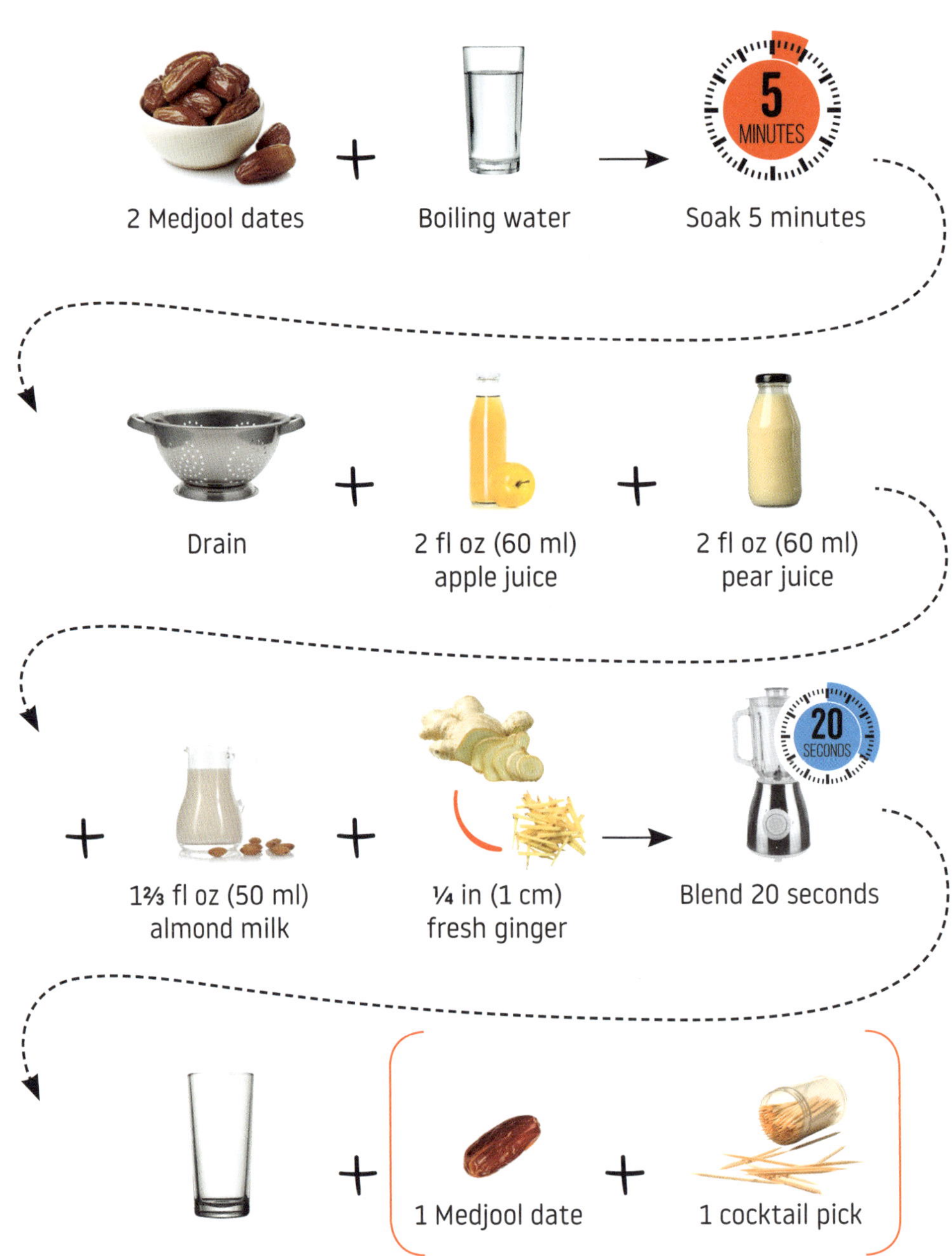

2 Medjool dates
+
Boiling water
5 MINUTES
Soak 5 minutes
Drain
+
2 fl oz (60 ml) apple juice
+
2 fl oz (60 ml) pear juice
+
1⅔ fl oz (50 ml) almond milk
+
¼ in (1 cm) fresh ginger
20 SECONDS
Blend 20 seconds
+
1 Medjool date
+
1 cocktail pick

MAKES 1 GLASS
PREPARATION: 10 MINUTES

- 3 Medjool dates
- 2 fl oz (60 ml) apple juice
- 2 fl oz (60 ml) pear juice
- 1⅔ fl oz (50 ml) almond milk
- ¼ in (1 cm) fresh ginger

81 CRUNCHY COLOMBO-COCONUT *nut mix*

2 fl oz (60 ml) maple syrup

\+

2 tablespoons apple cider vinegar

→

Bring to a boil

\+

1 oz (30 g) coconut oil

Melt

\+

1.5 tablespoons Colombo spice mix

\+

3½ oz (100 g) pecans

\+

3½ oz (100 g) cashews

\+

3½ oz (100 g) almonds

\+

1⅓ oz (40 g) coconut flakes

\+

2 oz (60 g) pepitas

→

Baking paper

\+

\+

1 teaspoon fleur de sel or sea salt

→

20
MINUTES

In the oven, at 320°F (160°C) 20 minutes

SERVES 8
PREPARATION: 10 MINUTES
COOKING: 25 MINUTES

- 2 fl oz (60 ml) maple syrup
- 2 tablespoons apple cider vinegar
- 1 oz (30 ml) coconut oil
- 1.5 tablespoons Colombo spice mix
- 3½ oz (100 g) pecans
- 3½ oz (100 g) cashews
- 3½ oz (100 g) almonds
- 1⅓ oz (40 g) coconut flakes
- 2 oz (60 g) pepitas
- 1 teaspoon fleur de sel or sea salt

82 GREEN TAPENADE

with almonds

7 oz (200 g)
green olives
2 garlic cloves
4 tablespoons
olive oil
½ lemon, juiced
½ bunch basil
Blend
1¾ oz (50 g)
almond meal
Blend
2 tablespoons
flaked almonds
5
MINUTES
Toast 5 minutes

SERVES 6
PREPARATION: 10 MINUTES
COOKING: 5 MINUTES
• 7 oz (200 g) green olives, pitted
• 2 garlic cloves
• 4 tablespoon olive oil
• ½ lemon, juiced
• ½ bunch basil
• 1¾ oz (50 g) almond meal
• 2 tablespoons flaked almonds

83 SARDINES *with grapefruit*

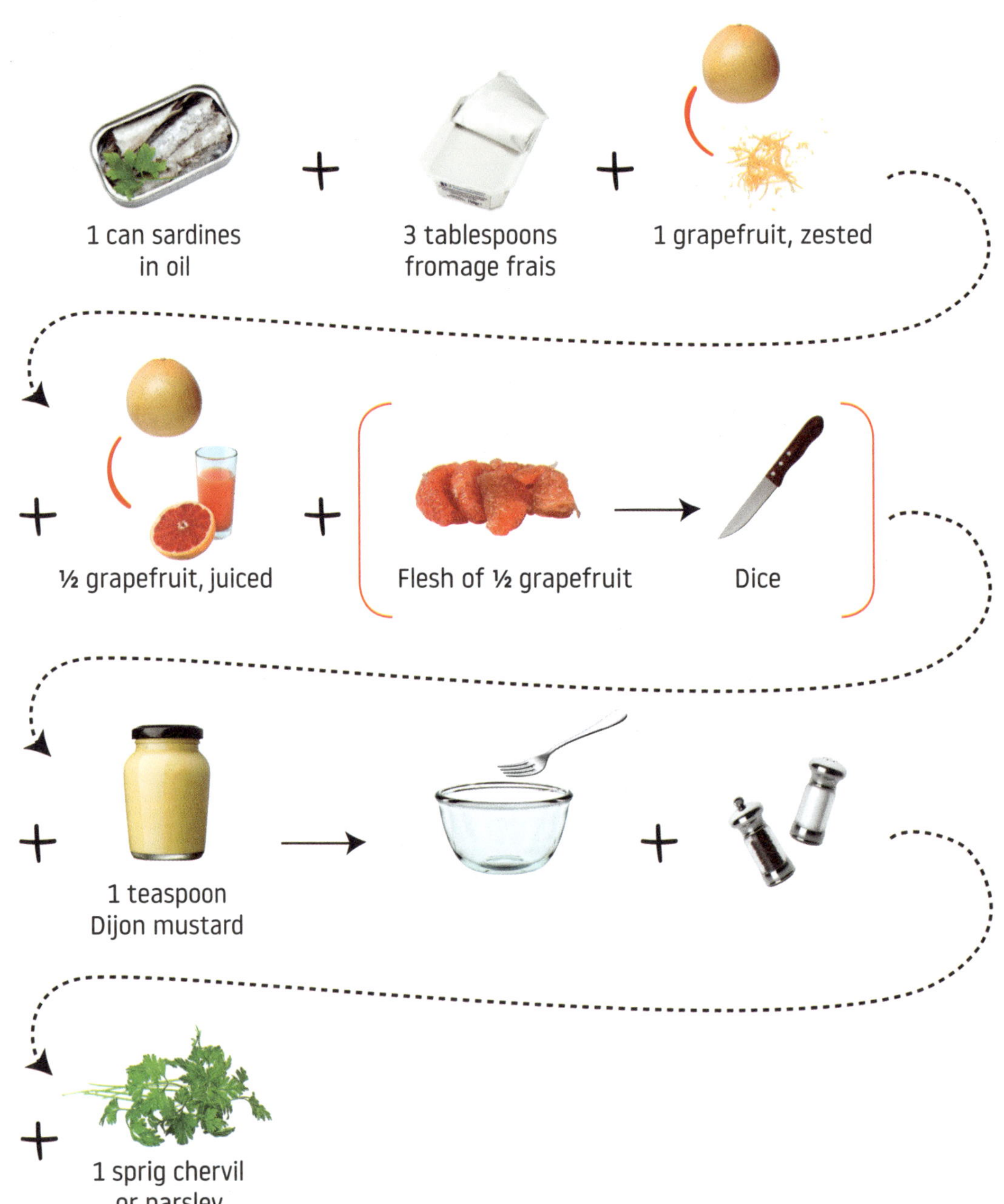

1 can sardines in oil
3 tablespoons fromage frais
1 grapefruit, zested
½ grapefruit, juiced
Flesh of ½ grapefruit
Dice
1 teaspoon Dijon mustard
1 sprig chervil or parsley

SERVES 4
PREPARATION: 5 MINUTES

- 1 can sardines in oil
- 3 tablespoons fromage frais
- 1 grapefruit, zested +
  ½ grapefruit, juiced +
  ½ grapefruit, diced
- 1 teaspoon Dijon mustard
- 1 sprig chervil or parsley

84 FISH *pâté*

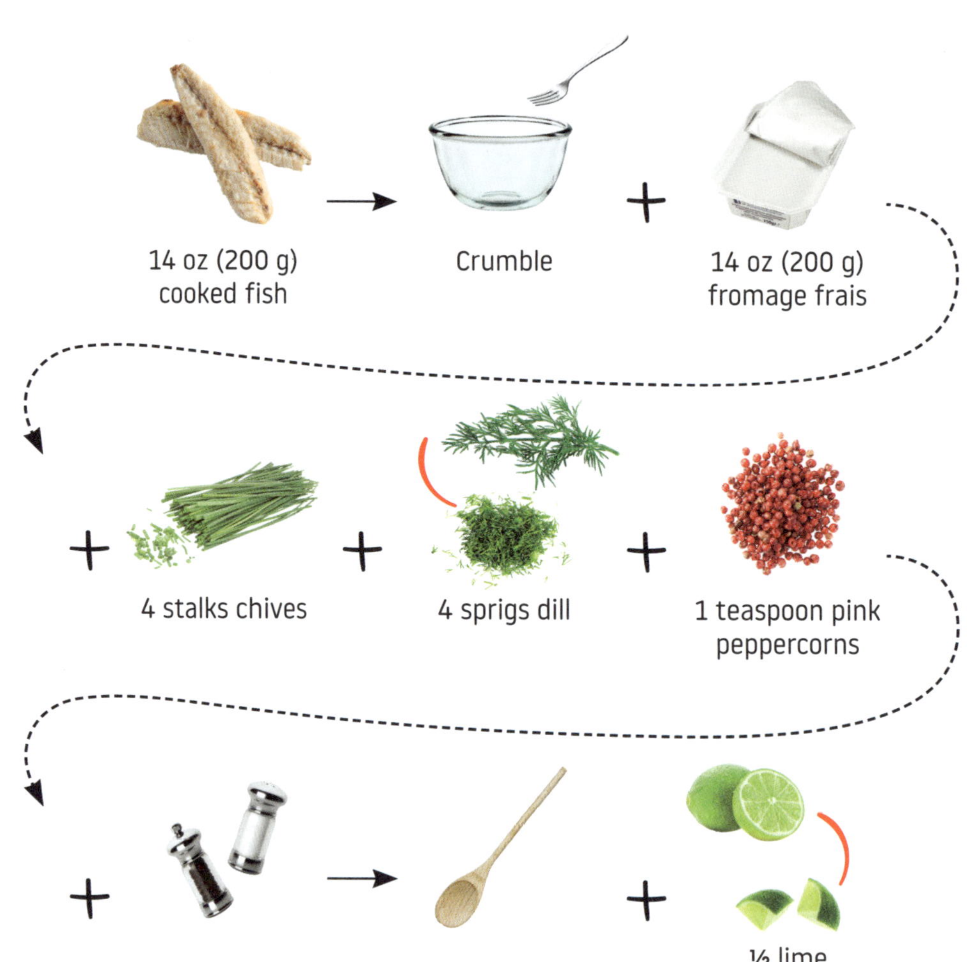
14 oz (200 g)
cooked fish
Crumble
14 oz (200 g)
fromage frais
4 stalks chives
4 sprigs dill
1 teaspoon pink
peppercorns
½ lime

MAKES 400 G PÂTÉ
PREPARATION: 5 MINUTES
• 14 oz (200 g) cooked fish such as tuna, mackerel or sardines
• 14 oz (200 g) fromage frais
• 4 stalks chives
• 4 sprigs dill
• 1 teaspoon pink peppercorns
• salt and pepper
• ½ lime, sliced`

85 TUNA TARTARE
with ginger

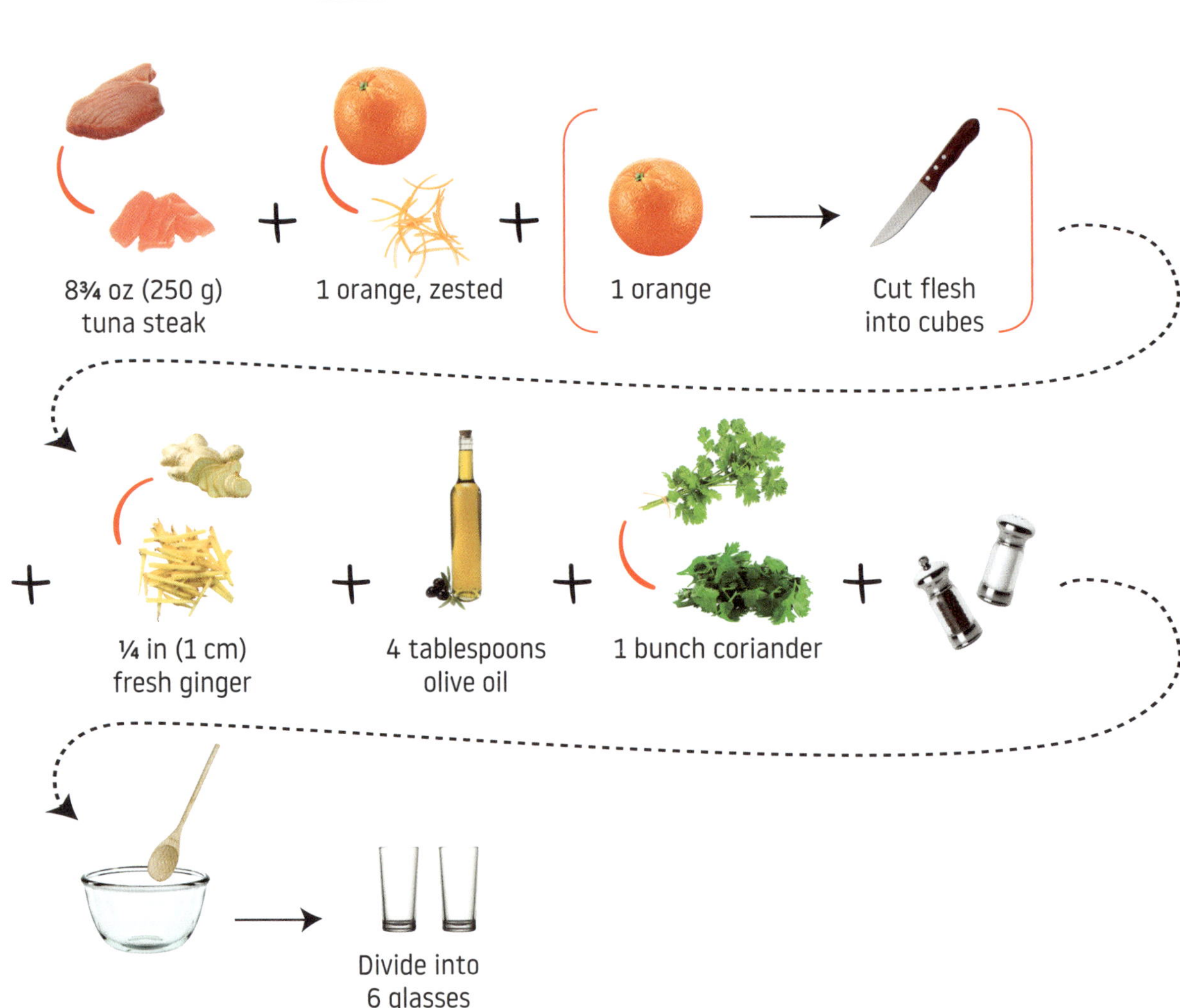

8¾ oz (250 g)
tuna steak
+
1 orange, zested
+
1 orange
Cut flesh
into cubes
+
¼ in (1 cm)
fresh ginger
+
4 tablespoons
olive oil
+
1 bunch coriander
+
Divide into
6 glasses

SERVES 6
PREPARATION: 15 MINUTES

- 8¾ oz (250 g) tuna steak
- 1 orange, zested and flesh cubed
- ¼ in (1 cm) fresh ginger, grated
- 4 tablespoons olive oil
- 1 bunch coriander
- salt and pepper

86 SMOKED TROUT
blinis

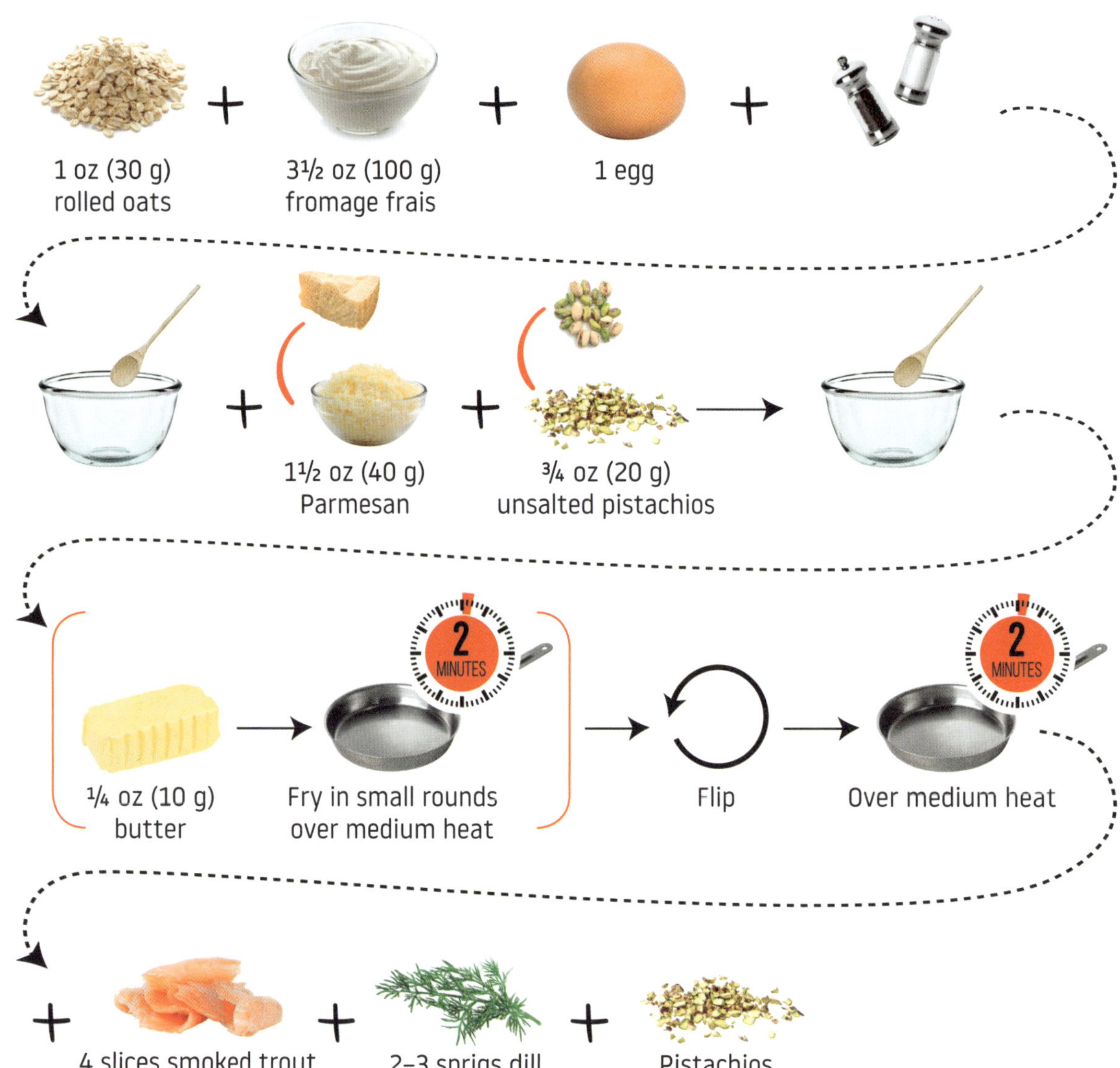

1 oz (30 g)
rolled oats
3½ oz (100 g)
fromage frais
1 egg
1½ oz (40 g)
Parmesan
¾ oz (20 g)
unsalted pistachios
2
MINUTES
¼ oz (10 g)
butter
Fry in small rounds
over medium heat
Flip
2
MINUTES
Over medium heat
4 slices smoked trout
2–3 sprigs dill
Pistachios

SERVES 4
PREPARATION: 10 MINUTES
COOKING: 10 MINUTES

- 1 oz (30 g) rolled oats
- 3½ oz (100 g) fromage frais
- 1 egg
- salt and pepper to taste
- 1½ oz (40 g) Parmesan, grated
- ¾ oz (20 g) unsalted pistachios, finely chopped + extra to decorate
- ¼ oz (10 g) butter
- 4 slices smoked trout, cut into small pieces
- 2–3 sprigs dill

87 LOMO CROSTINI

and artichoke pesto

1 jar artichoke hearts
Drain
Blend
1 handful basil leaves
½ lemon, juiced
Blend in short bursts
4 tablespoons olive oil, added gradually
12 slices baguette
Toast
12–24 thin slices dried lomo or prosciutto
1 drizzle olive oil
A few basil leaves

SERVES 4–6
PREPARATION: 20 MINUTES

- 1 jar artichoke hearts
- 1 handful basil leaves + a few leaves
- ½ lemon, juiced
- salt and pepper
- 4 tablespoons olive oil + 1 drizzle
- 12 slices baguette
- 12–24 thin slices dried lomo or prosciutto

88 TOMATO BITES

with fromage frais and herbs

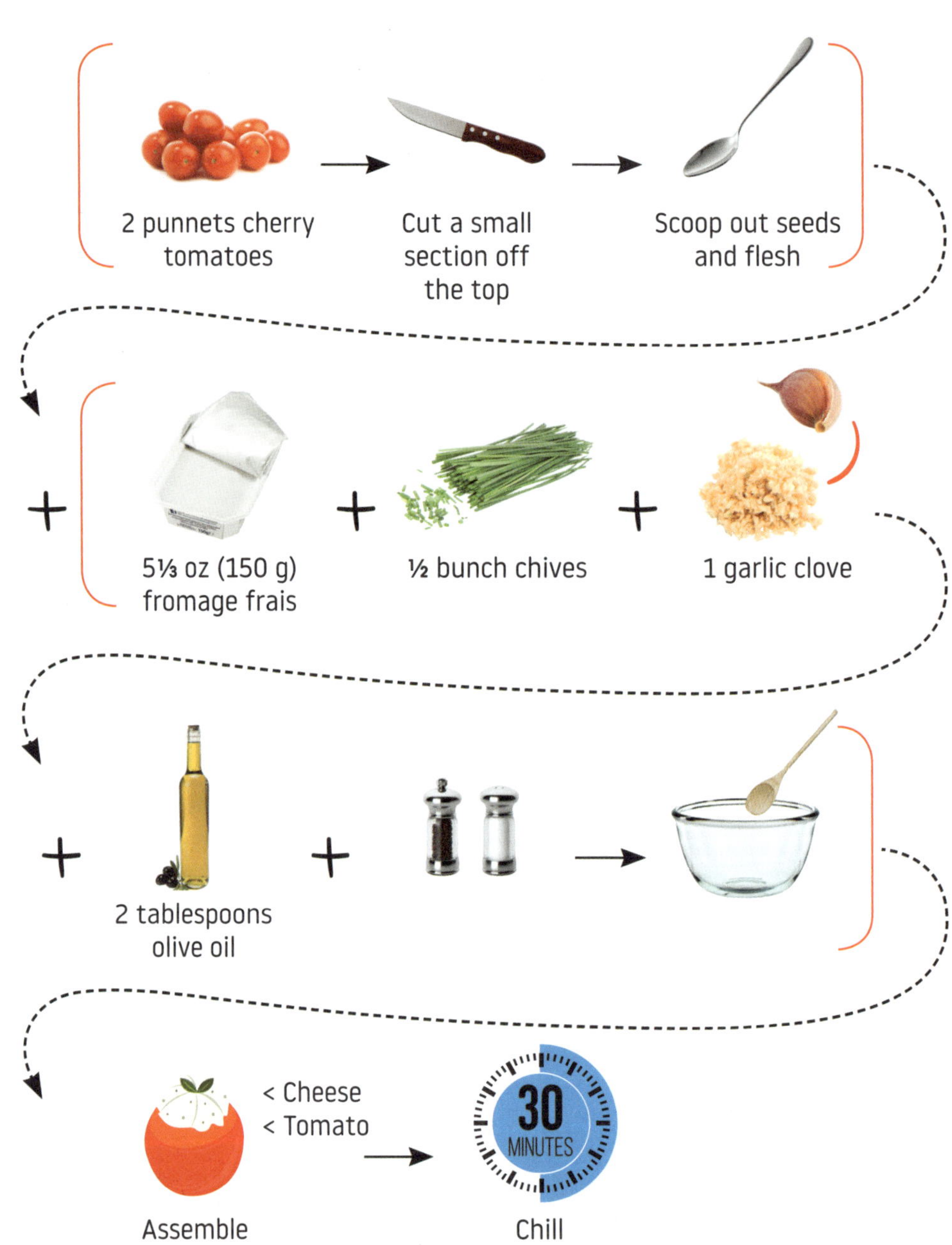

2 punnets cherry tomatoes
Cut a small section off the top
Scoop out seeds and flesh
5⅓ oz (150 g) fromage frais
½ bunch chives
1 garlic clove
2 tablespoons olive oil
< Cheese
< Tomato
Assemble
30 MINUTES
Chill

SERVES 4–6
PREPARATION: 15 MINUTES
CHILLING: 30 MINUTES

- 2 punnets cherry tomatoes
- 5⅓ oz (150 g) fromage frais
- ½ bunch chives, chopped
- 1 garlic clove, minced
- 2 tablespoons olive oil
- salt and pepper

89 MUSHROOM
macarons

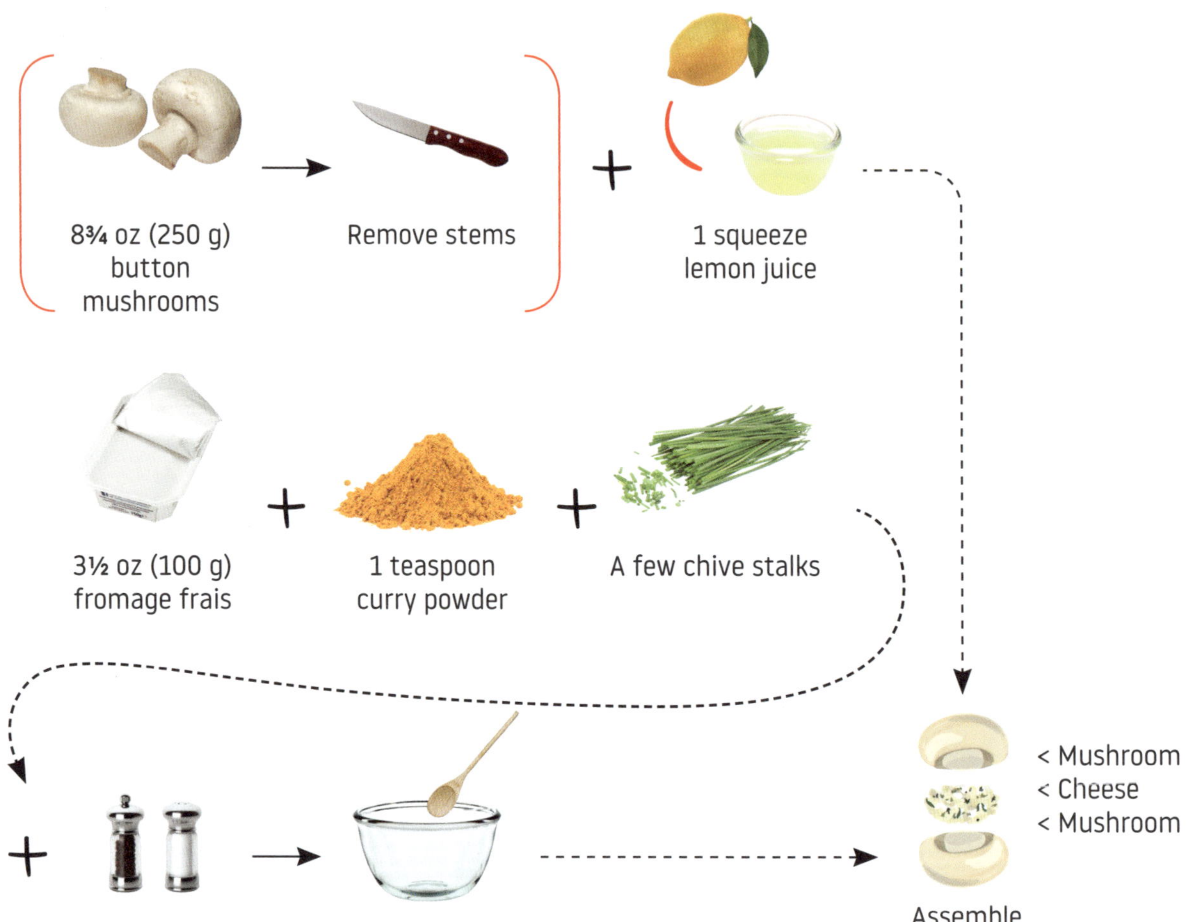
8¾ oz (250 g)
button
mushrooms
Remove stems
1 squeeze
lemon juice
3½ oz (100 g)
fromage frais
1 teaspoon
curry powder
A few chive stalks
< Mushroom
< Cheese
< Mushroom
Assemble

SERVES 6
PREPARATION: 10 MINUTES

- 8¾ oz (250 g) button mushrooms
- 1 squeeze lemon juice
- 3½ oz (100 g) fromage frais
- 1 teaspoon curry powder
- a few chive stalks, chopped

90 JAMÓN *breadsticks*

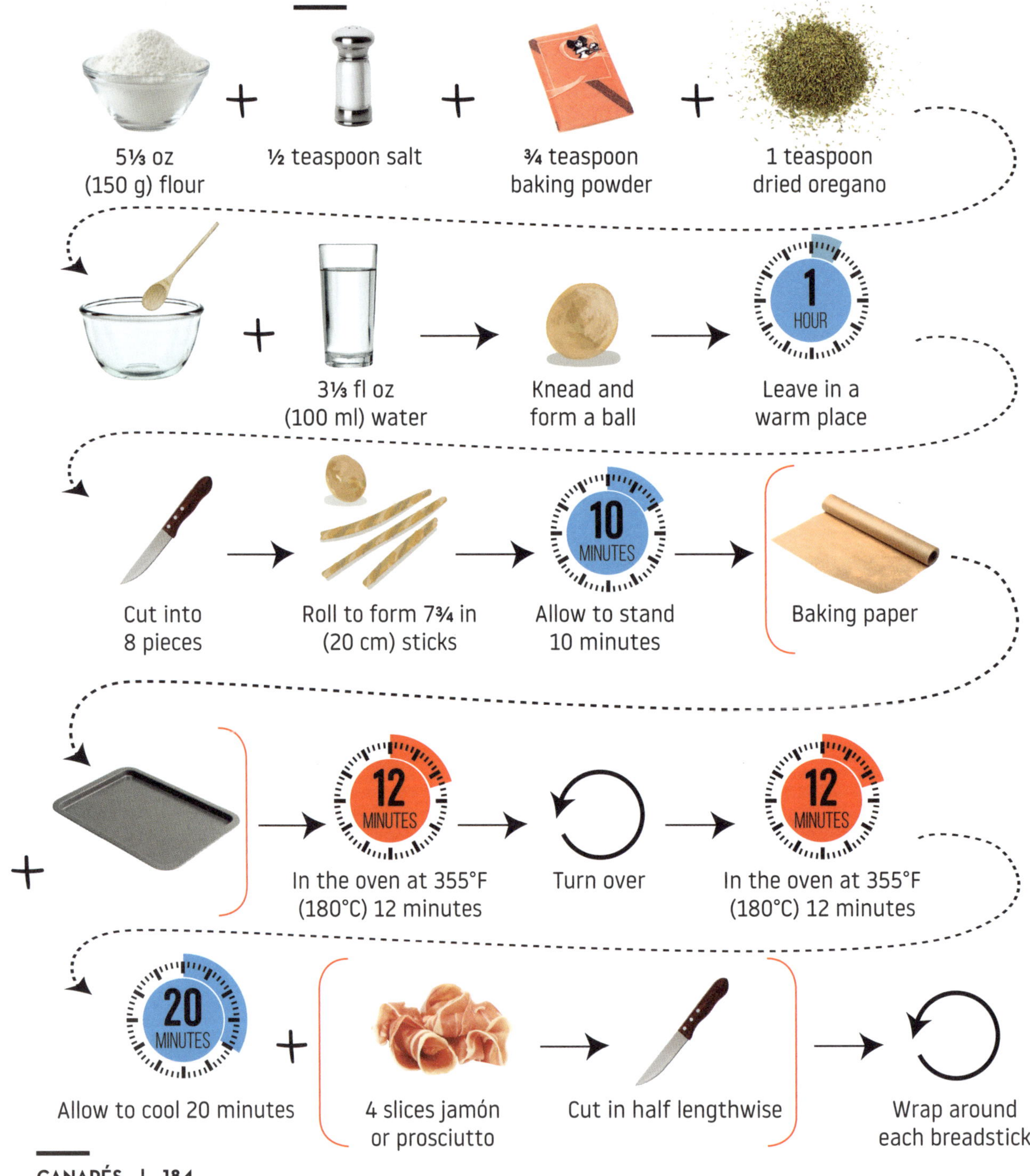
5⅓ oz
(150 g) flour
½ teaspoon salt
¾ teaspoon
baking powder
1 teaspoon
dried oregano
3⅓ fl oz
(100 ml) water
Knead and
form a ball
1
HOUR
Leave in a
warm place
Cut into
8 pieces
Roll to form 7¾ in
(20 cm) sticks
10
MINUTES
Allow to stand
10 minutes
Baking paper
12
MINUTES
In the oven at 355°F
(180°C) 12 minutes
Turn over
12
MINUTES
In the oven at 355°F
(180°C) 12 minutes
20
MINUTES
Allow to cool 20 minutes
4 slices jamón
or prosciutto
Cut in half lengthwise
Wrap around
each breadstick

SERVES 4
PREPARATION: 10 MINUTES
RESTING: 70 MINUTES
COOKING: 24 MINUTES

- 5⅓ oz (150 g) flour
- ½ teaspoon salt
- ¾ teaspoon baking powder
- 1 teaspoon dried oregano
- 3⅓ fl oz (100 ml) water
- 4 slices jamón or prosciutto

91 CHERRY TOMATOES

toffee apple style

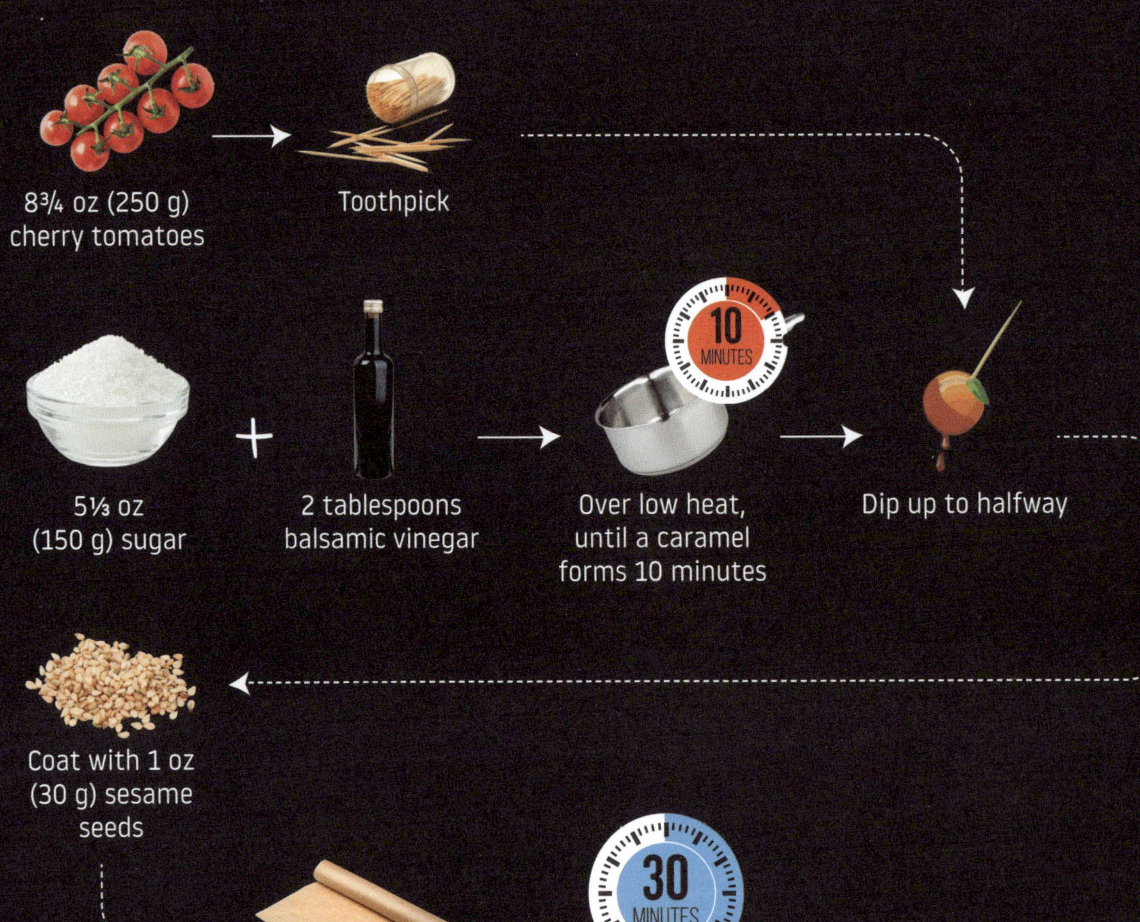
8¾ oz (250 g)
cherry tomatoes
Toothpick
10
MINUTES
5⅓ oz
(150 g) sugar
+
2 tablespoons
balsamic vinegar
Over low heat,
until a caramel
forms 10 minutes
Dip up to halfway
Coat with 1 oz
(30 g) sesame
seeds
30
MINUTES

Baking paper

Allow to cool
30 minutes

SERVES 4
PREPARATION: 15 MINUTES
COOKING: 10 MINUTES
RESTING: 30 MINUTES

- 8¾ oz (250 g) cherry tomatoes
- 5⅓ oz (150 g) sugar
- 2 tablespoons balsamic vinegar
- 1 oz (30 g) sesame seeds

92 CHEESE AND BACON *pops*

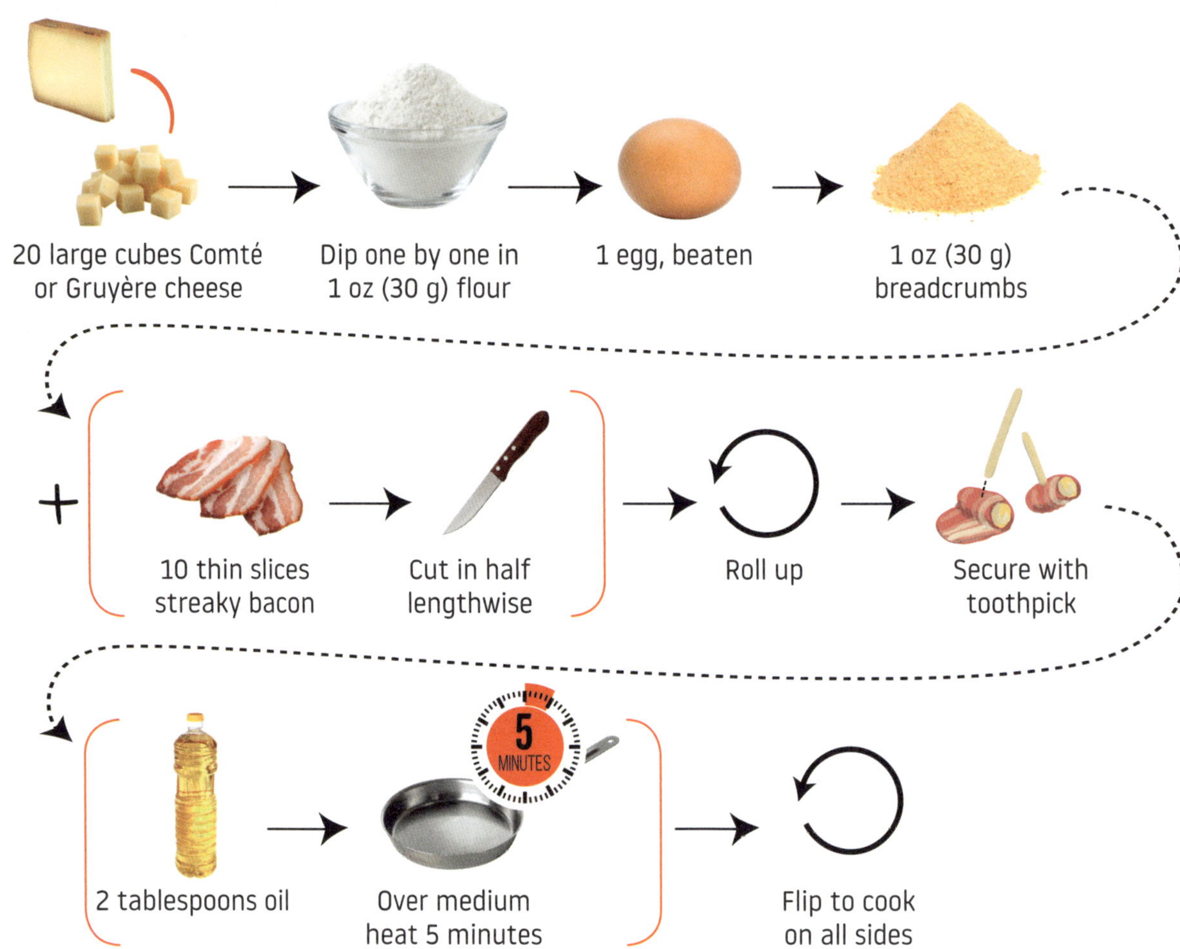

20 large cubes Comté
or Gruyère cheese
Dip one by one in
1 oz (30 g) flour
1 egg, beaten
1 oz (30 g)
breadcrumbs
+
10 thin slices
streaky bacon
Cut in half
lengthwise
Roll up
Secure with
toothpick
2 tablespoons oil
5
MINUTES
Over medium
heat 5 minutes
Flip to cook
on all sides

SERVES 6
PREPARATION: 10 MINUTES
COOKING: 5 MINUTES

- 20 large cubes Comté or Gruyère cheese
- 1 oz (30 g) flour
- 1 egg, beaten
- 1 oz (30 g) breadcrumbs
- 10 thin slices streaky bacon
- 2 tablespoons oil

93 CRUMBED PRAWNS
with wasabi

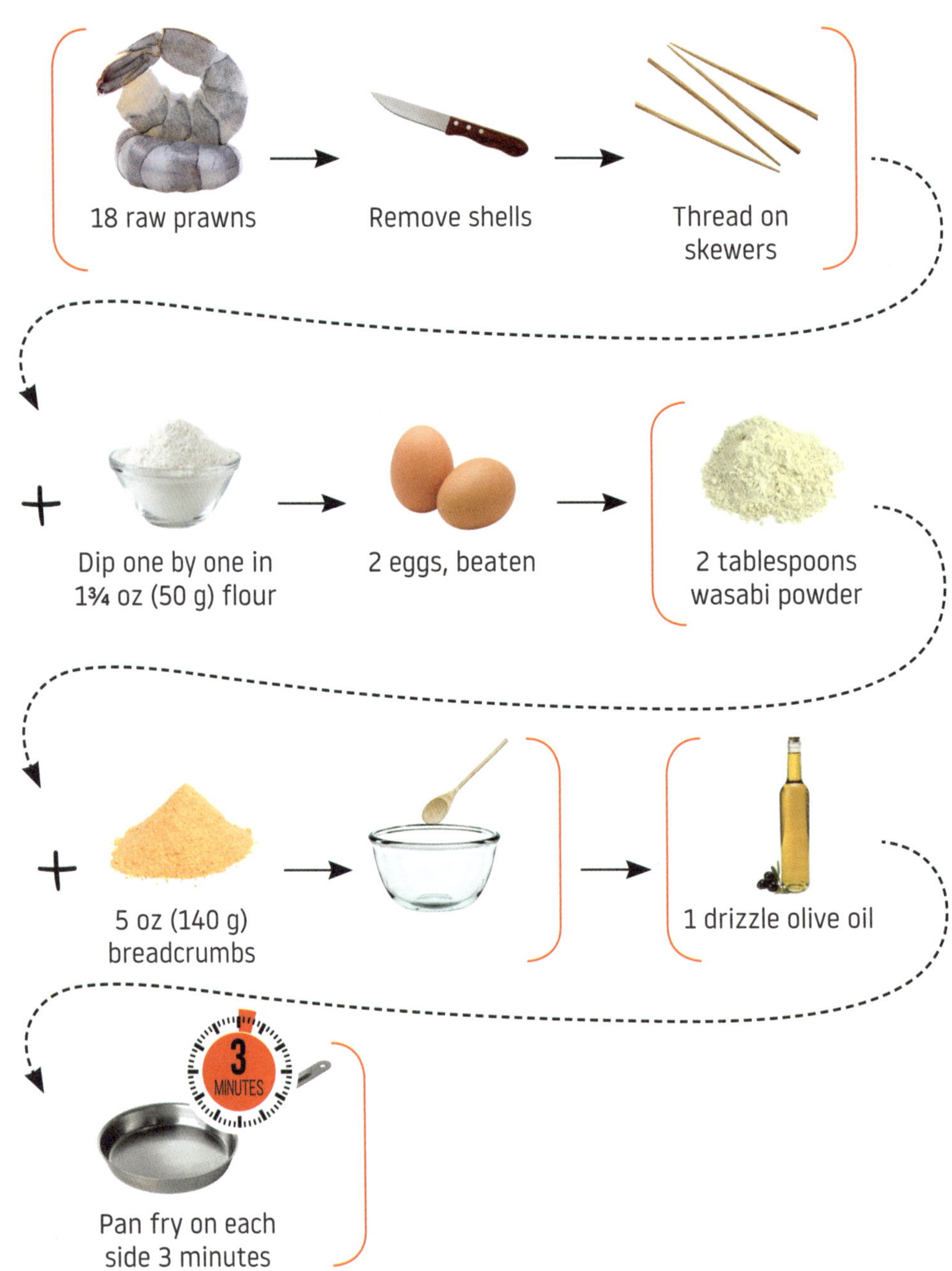

18 raw prawns
Remove shells
Thread on skewers
Dip one by one in 1¾ oz (50 g) flour
2 eggs, beaten
2 tablespoons wasabi powder
5 oz (140 g) breadcrumbs
1 drizzle olive oil
3 MINUTES
Pan fry on each side 3 minutes

SERVES 6
PREPARATION: 15 MINUTES
COOKING: 6 MINUTES

- 18 raw prawns
- 1¾ oz (50 g) flour
- 2 eggs, beaten
- 2 tablespoons wasabi powder
- 5 oz (140 g) breadcrumbs
- 1 drizzle olive oil

94 VEAL MEATBALLS
with spinach and gorgonzola

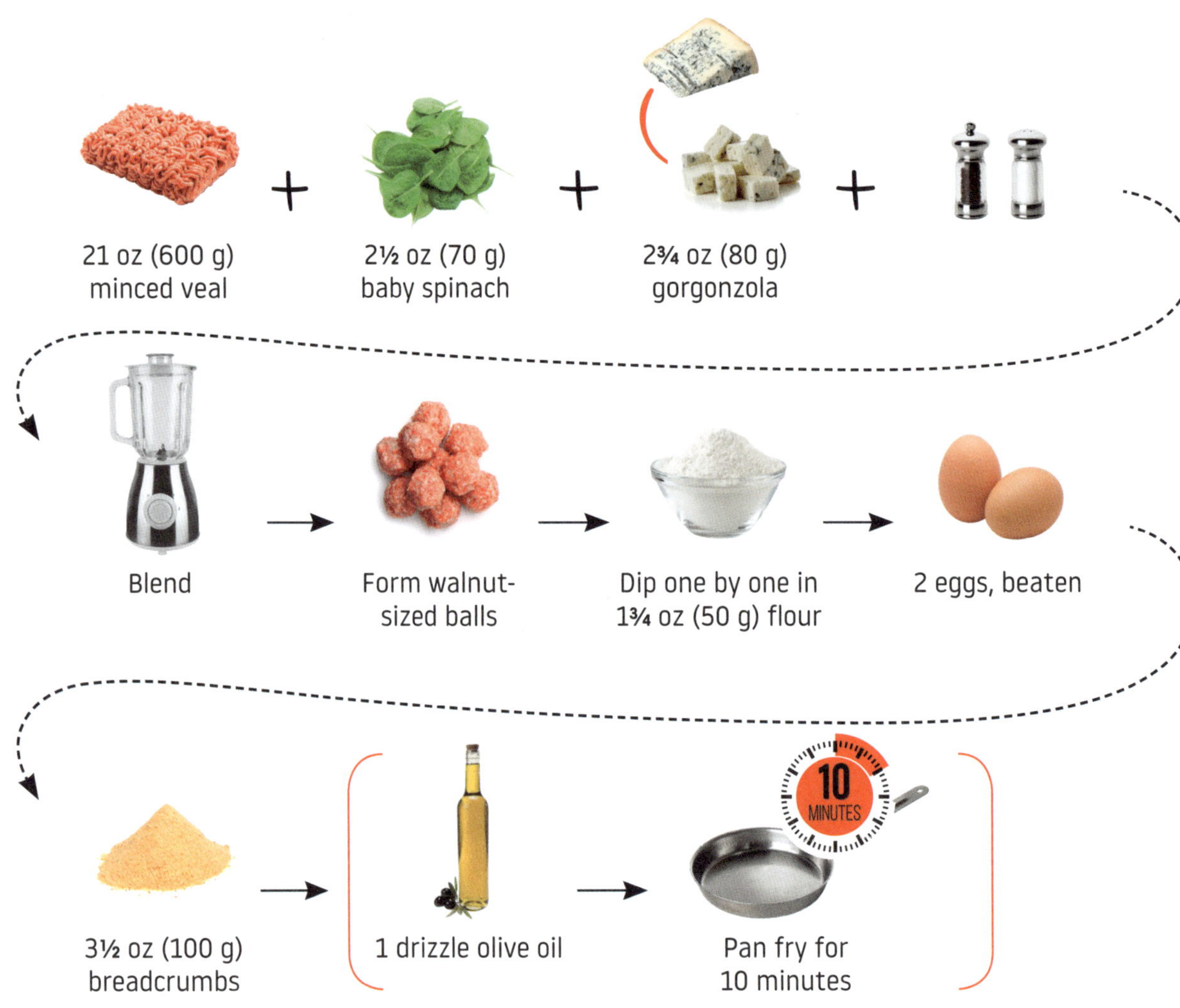
21 oz (600 g)
minced veal
2½ oz (70 g)
baby spinach
2¾ oz (80 g)
gorgonzola
Blend
Form walnut-
sized balls
Dip one by one in
1¾ oz (50 g) flour
2 eggs, beaten
3½ oz (100 g)
breadcrumbs
1 drizzle olive oil
10
MINUTES
Pan fry for
10 minutes

SERVES 6
PREPARATION: 15 MINUTES
COOKING: 10 MINUTES

- 21 oz (600 g) minced veal
- 2½ oz (70 g) baby spinach
- 2¾ oz (80 g) gorgonzola
- salt and pepper
- 1¾ oz (50 g) flour
- 2 eggs, beaten
- 3½ oz (100 g) breadcrumbs
- 1 drizzle olive oil

95 OVEN-BAKED *falafels*

17½ oz (500 g) tinned chickpeas

½ bunch parsley

1 onion

1 garlic clove

Blend

1 teaspoon ground cumin

1 tablespoon breadcrumbs

+

Form balls

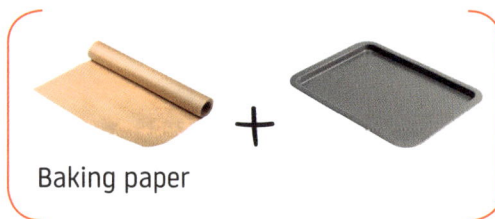

→ →

Baking paper

+

+

1 drizzle olive oil

→

25
MINUTES

In the oven at 355°F (180°C) 25 minutes

SERVES 4
PREPARATION: 15 MINUTES
COOKING: 25 MINUTES

- 17½ oz (500 g) tinned chickpeas, drained
- ½ bunch parsley
- 1 onion, diced
- 1 garlic clove, minced
- 1 teaspoon ground cumin
- 1 tablespoon breadcrumbs
- salt and pepper
- 1 drizzle olive oil

96 TARTS
with onion and goat's cheese

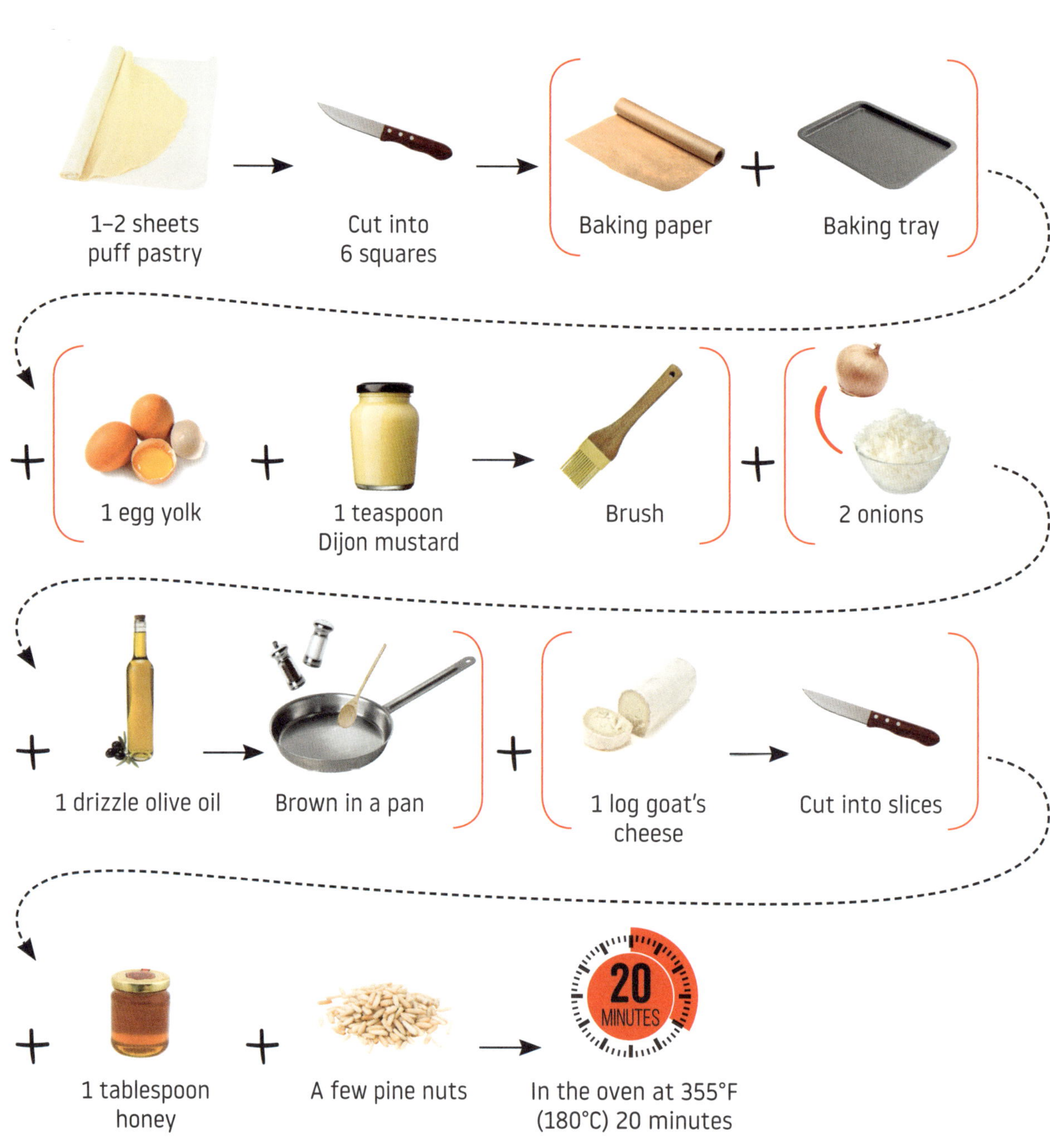
1–2 sheets puff pastry
Cut into 6 squares
Baking paper
Baking tray
1 egg yolk
1 teaspoon Dijon mustard
Brush
2 onions
1 drizzle olive oil
Brown in a pan
1 log goat's cheese
Cut into slices
1 tablespoon honey
A few pine nuts
20 MINUTES
In the oven at 355°F (180°C) 20 minutes

SERVES 4
PREPARATION: 15 MINUTES
COOKING: 25 MINUTES

- 1–2 sheets puff pastry
- 1 egg yolk
- 1 teaspoon Dijon mustard
- 2 onions, diced
- 1 drizzle olive oil
- 1 log goat's cheese
- 1 tablespoon honey
- a few pine nuts

97 HEDGEHOG BREAD

with three cheeses

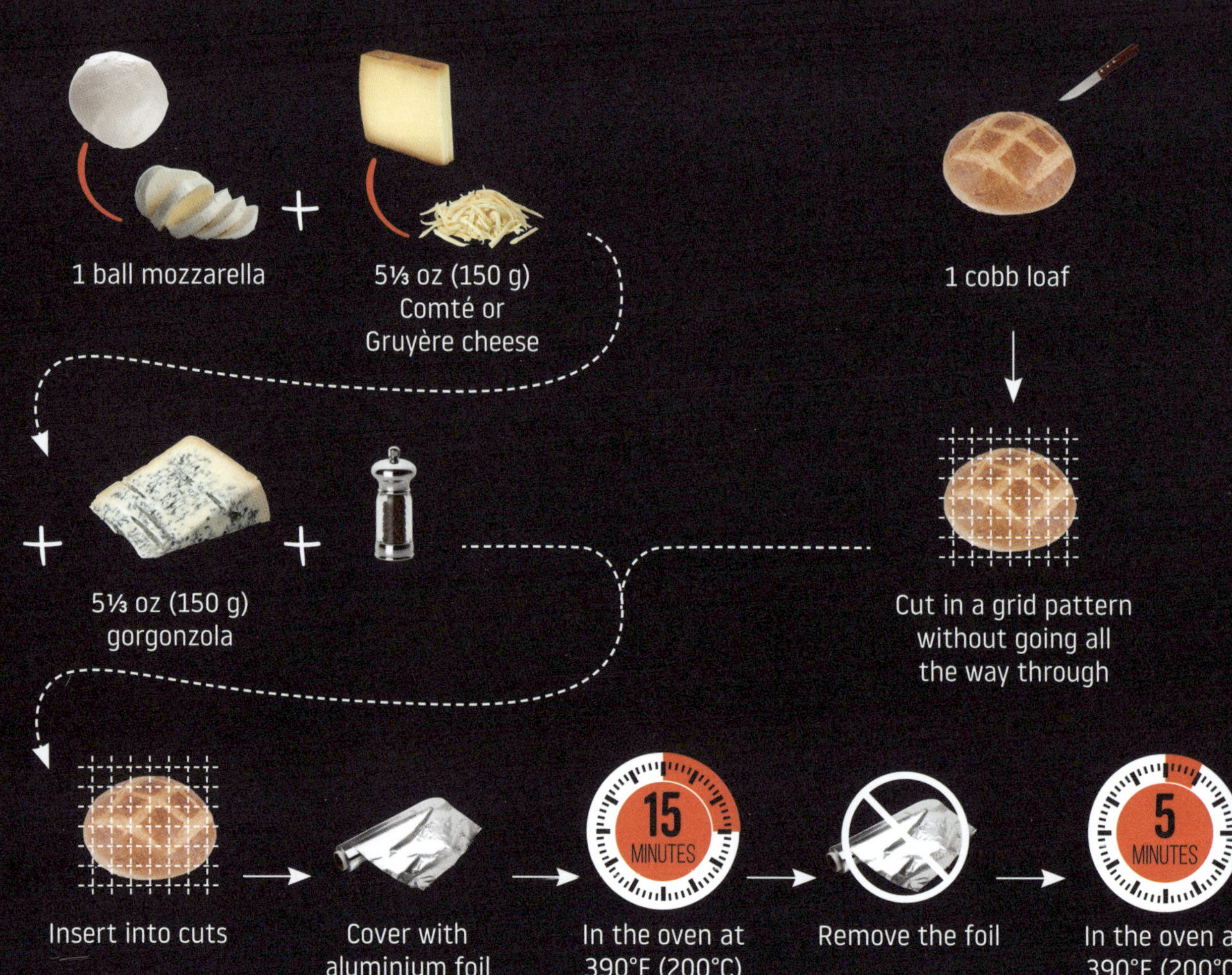

1 ball mozzarella
5⅓ oz (150 g)
Comté or
Gruyère cheese
1 cobb loaf
5⅓ oz (150 g)
gorgonzola
Cut in a grid pattern
without going all
the way through
Insert into cuts
Cover with
aluminium foil
15
MINUTES
In the oven at
390°F (200°C)
15 minutes
Remove the foil
5
MINUTES
In the oven a
390°F (200°C
5 minutes

SERVES 4
PREPARATION: 15 MINUTES
COOKING: 20 MINUTES

- 1 cob loaf, cut in a grid pattern without going all the way through
- 1 ball mozzarella, sliced
- 5⅓ oz (150 g) Comté or Gruyère cheese, grated
- 5⅓ oz (150 g) gorgonzola, crumbled
- pepper

98 PIZZA *pops*

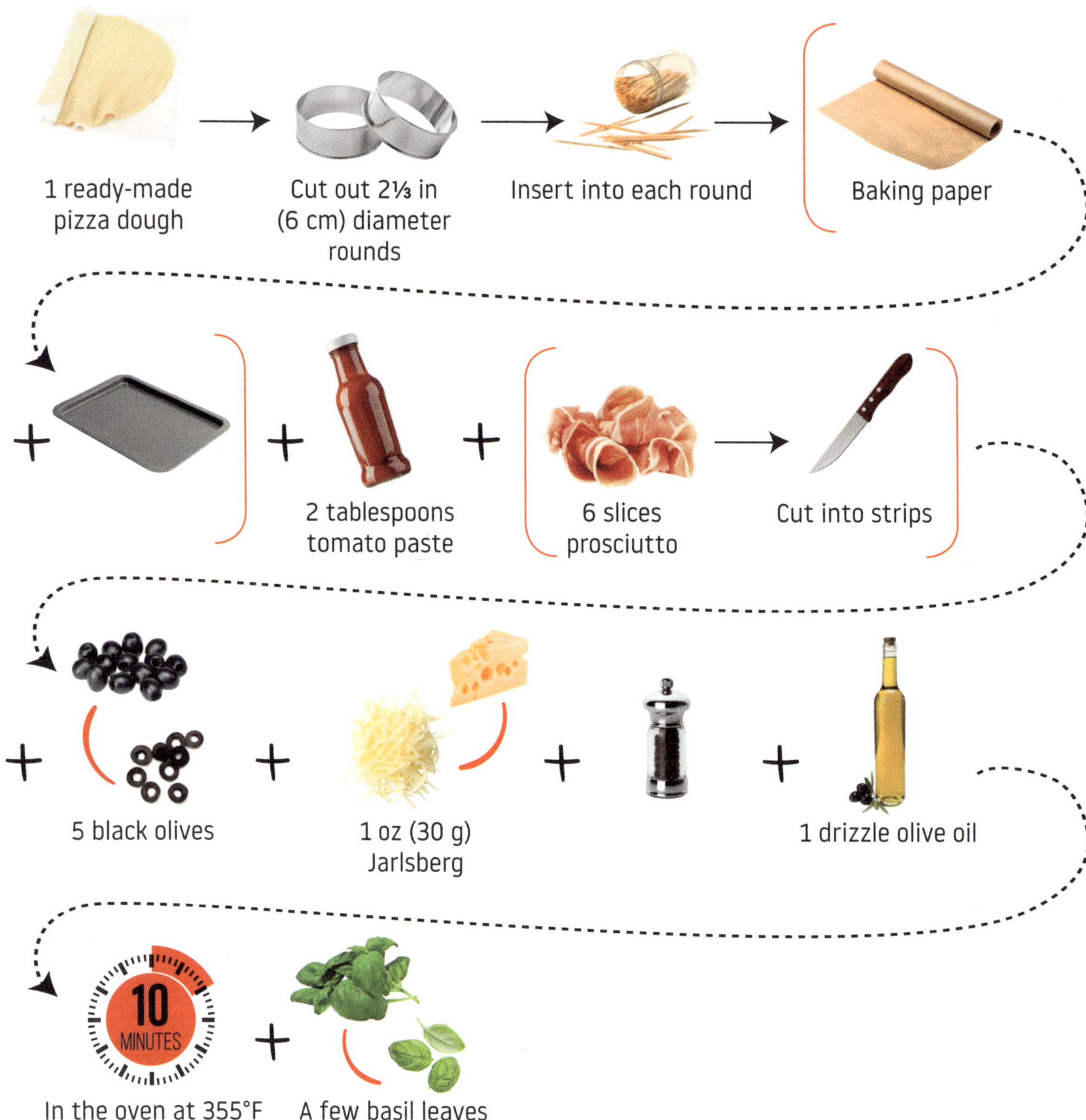

1 ready-made pizza dough
Cut out 2⅓ in (6 cm) diameter rounds
Insert into each round
Baking paper
2 tablespoons tomato paste
6 slices prosciutto
Cut into strips
5 black olives
1 oz (30 g) Jarlsberg
1 drizzle olive oil
10 MINUTES
In the oven at 355°F (180°C) 10 minutes
A few basil leaves

SERVES 4
PREPARATION: 15 MINUTES
COOKING: 10 MINUTES

- 1 ready-made pizza dough
- 2 tablespoons tomato paste
- 6 slices prosciutto
- 5 black olives, pitted and sliced
- 1 oz (30 g) Jarlsberg
- pepper
- 1 drizzle olive oil
- a few basil leaves

99 SCROLLS WITH HAM, MUSTARD *and cheese*

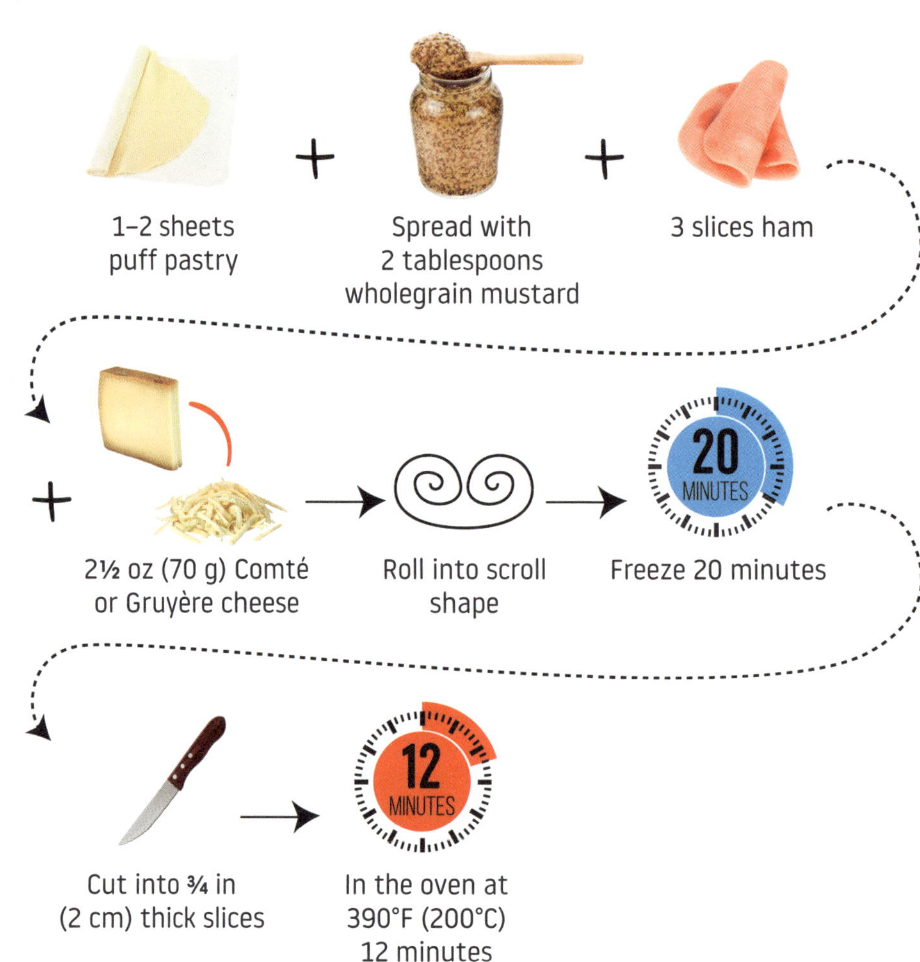
1–2 sheets puff pastry
Spread with 2 tablespoons wholegrain mustard
3 slices ham
2½ oz (70 g) Comté or Gruyère cheese
Roll into scroll shape
20 MINUTES
Freeze 20 minutes
Cut into ¾ in (2 cm) thick slices
12 MINUTES
In the oven at 390°F (200°C) 12 minutes

SERVES 6
PREPARATION: 15 MINUTES
FREEZING: 20 MINUTES
COOKING: 12 MINUTES

- 1–2 sheets puff pastry
- 2 tablespoons wholegrain mustard
- 3 slices ham, chopped
- 2½ oz (70 g) Comté or Gruyère cheese, grated

100 ROQUEFORT BAGUETTE

with walnuts

1 baguette
Cut off the top and remove some of the flesh
10½ oz (300 g) fromage frais
5⅓ oz (150 g) Roquefort or blue cheese
2 oz (60 g) walnuts
1 drizzle olive oil
< Cheese
< Bread
Assemble
15
MINUTES

Wrap in baking paper

In the oven at 355°F (180°C) 15 minutes

1 tablespoon chives

SERVES 4–6
PREPARATION: 10 MINUTES
COOKING: 15 MINUTES
• 1 baguette
• 10½ oz (300 g) fromage frais
• 5⅓ oz (150 g) Roquefort or blue cheese, crumbled
• 2 oz (60 g) walnuts, chopped
• 1 drizzle olive oil
• 1 tablespoon chives, chopped

101 SUN TART

with tapenade and ricotta

1 sheet puff pastry
Spread 2 tablespoons tapenade up to ¾ in / 2 cm from the edge
8¾ oz (250 g) fresh ricotta
Cover with another puff pastry sheet
Place a glass upside down in the centre of the pastry
Cut into 4, then 8, then 16
1 egg yolk
1 tablespoon water
Brush
Twist each strip
30 MINUTES
In the oven at 355°F (180°C) 30 minutes
A few sprigs of thyme

SERVES 4–6
PREPARATION: 10 MINUTES
COOKING: 30 MINUTES

- 2 sheets puff pastry, cut in circles
- 2 tablespoons tapenade
- 8¾ oz (250 g) fresh ricotta
- 1 egg yolk
- a few sprigs of thyme

RECIPE INDEX BY INGREDIENTS

ALPHABETICAL RECIPE INDEX

A Gelding Street Press book
An imprint of Rockpool Publishing
PO Box 252, Summer Hill
NSW 2130 Australia

geldingstreetpress.com
Follow us! Geldingstreet_press

First published by Larousse as *Mocktails Sans Bla Bla*
under ISBN 9782036073272

This edition published in 2026 by Rockpool Publishing
ISBN: 9781922662378

RECIPE CREDITS © LAROUSSE

Berengere Abraham: 96; Vincent Amiel: 93, 94; Zoe Armbruster: 82; Séverine Augé: 14, 84; Anna Austry: 86; Blandine Boyer: 87; Catherine Conan: 90; Pauline Dubois-Platet: 99; Sandrine Houdré-Grégoire: 01, 02, 03, 04, 05, 06, 07, 08, 09, 10, 11, 13, 15, 17, 18, 19, 20, 21, 22, 23, 24, 27, 28, 29, 31, 32, 33, 35, 37, 38, 39, 41, 42, 43, 44, 46, 47, 48, 49, 50, 51, 52, 53, 54, 55, 57, 58, 59, 60, 61, 63, 64, 65, 66, 67, 68, 72, 76, 77, 78, 79, 80 ; Sandrine Houdré-Grégoire and Régis Célabe: 36, 70; Sandrine Houdré-Grégoire and Matthias Giroud : 25, 26, 34, 45, 56, 62, 69, 73, 74; Sandrine Houdré-Grégoire and Guillaume Guerbois: 12, 30, 30, 40, 71, 75; Guillaume Guerbois: 16; Coralie Ferreira : 81; Delphine Lebrun: 89, 91, 95, 97, 100; Mélanie Martin: 88, 98; Aude Royer: 92; Noémie Strouk: 83, 85.

PHOTOGRAPHY CREDITS © LAROUSSE

Delphine Amar-Constantini: 90; Fabrice Besse: 13, 16, 17, 18, 20, 22, 27, 28, 31, 36, 38, 41, 43, 46, 49, 54, 61, 63, 64, 65, 66, 68, 70, 72, 76, 77, 78, 79, 80; Emanuela Cino: 87, 92; Charly Deslandes: 01, 02, 03, 04, 05, 06, 07, 08, 09, 10, 11, 12, 14, 15, 19, 21, 23, 24, 29, 30, 32, 33, 35, 37, 39, 40, 42, 44, 47, 48, 50, 51, 52, 53, 55, 57, 58, 59, 60, 67, 71, 75, 81, 84, 96 ; Loran Dhérines: 25; Sophie Dumont: 89, 91, 95, 97, 100; Blaise Gargadennec: 82; Marie-José Jarry: 26, 34, 45, 56, 62, 74; Céline Mermet-Bouvier: 86; Claire Payen: 93, 94; Olivier Ploton: 69, 73, 83, 85; Aline Princet: 88, 98; Fabrice Veigas: 99.

Images of ingredients and utensils © Shutterstock

Cover images © Shutterstock

Cover design by Christine Armstrong, Rockpool Publishing
Translated by Nicola Thayil
Translation edited by Lisa Macken

Printed and bound in China
10 9 8 7 6 5 4 3 2 1